POEMS TO ENJOY: BOOK TWO

Chosen and Edited by Verner Bickley

Proverse Hong Kong

VERNER BICKLEY, MBE, PhD, is a well-known "voice", educationist, and adjudicator, who has held director-level positions in Universities and Government Departments. He is Chairman Emeritus of the English-Speaking Union (HK) and Co-Founder of the International Proverse Prizes for unpublished writing. He travels frequently to judge public-speaking competitions and regularly adjudicates verse and prose speaking and reading, as well as drama and choral speaking.

Dr Bickley's series of graded poetry anthologies – **POEMS TO ENJOY** – is a well-established tool for learning and teaching English at all levels. Useful notes and a teaching guide are included.

Taken as a whole, this five-book series is suitable for all students, teachers and parents. **Book 1** can be used and enjoyed by Primary 1-3 students and **Book 2** by Primary 4-6 students. **Book 3** can be used and enjoyed by Secondary 1-2 students, **Book 4** by Secondary 3-4 students and **Book 5** by secondary 5-6 students. Students, parents and teachers will enjoy and find useful Dr Bickley's selection of poems.

It is strongly recommended that readers also purchase the Third Edition, which is accompanied by a CD containing lively readings of all poems in the book. These recordings assist pronunciation and help those preparing for solo verse speaking and reading, duo and group-work and choral-speaking in Speech Festivals. They also enhance reading experience.

Parents will welcome this book, in all editions, which gives them the opportunity to read aloud with their children.

~~ A PERENNIAL FAVOURITE ~~

POEMS TO ENJOY

BOOK TWO

AN ANTHOLOGY OF POEMS

FOR ADVANCED PRIMARY STUDENTS AND READERS

WITH TEACHING AND LEARNING NOTES AND GUIDE

CHOSEN AND EDITED BY DR VERNER BICKLEY, MBE, PhD (Lond.), MA, BA (Hons), DipEd, LRAM, LGSM, FCIL, FRSA

Proverse Hong Kong

Poems to Enjoy: Book Two.
Chosen and Edited by Verner Bickley.
With teaching and performance notes by Verner Bickley.

5th Edition published in Hong Kong by Proverse Hong Kong, February 2019
Copyright © Verner Bickley, February 2019.
ISBN: 978-988-8491-58-2

Distribution and other enquiries to: Proverse Hong Kong, P.O.Box 259,
Tung Chung Post Office, Tung Chung, Lantau, NT, Hong Kong SAR.
E-mail: proverse@netvigator.com   Web site: www.proversepublishing.com

Illustrations copyright © Proverse Hong Kong.
Page design by Proverse Hong Kong. Cover design, Proverse Hong Kong and Artist Hong Kong Company.

Poems to Enjoy: Book Two was first published in the United Kingdom in 1960, by University of London
Press Ltd, copyright © Verner Bickley 1960, with Teaching Notes in a separate volume.
Copyright © Verner Bickley 1960.
The 3rd ed. was published in pbk in Hong Kong by Proverse Hong Kong, with an audio recording on CD of
all poems in the anthology, June 2013. Copyright © Verner Bickley, June 2013. ISBN 978-988-8167-51-7.
Some of the poems in the third (as well as the first) edition of *Poems to Enjoy* Book 2
appeared in *Poems To Enjoy*, Book Two (2nd edition), which was part of a three-volume series.

Proverse Hong Kong

British Library Cataloguing in Publication Data (for 3rd edition, with audio CDs)

Poems to enjoy.
Book 2. -- 3rd ed.
1. English poetry. 2. Oral interpretation of poetry--
Juvenile literature. 3. English poetry--Study and teaching
(Elementary) 4. English language--Study and teaching--
Foreign speakers.
I. Bickley, Verner Courtenay.
821'.008-dc23

ISBN-13: 9789888167517

Acknowledgments

For permission to use copyright material thanks are due to: Miss Mary Daunt for her poem "Ducks"; Messrs. Blackie & Sons, Ltd. for "Strange Talk" by Lucy E. Yates and "The Frog and the Bird" by Vera Hessey; The Clarendon Press and Mr. James Nimmo for "Space Travellers" from *The Oxford Book of Verse for Juniors*, "The Fishes" by Lucy Diamond and "If You Have a Tabby-Cat" by A. G. Herbertson, both from *100 Poems for Children*; Messrs. Evans Brothers Limited for "The Magic Room" by Irene Thompson from *Child Education*; Messrs. William Heinemann Ltd. for "The Elephant" by Herbert Asquith from *Pillicock Hill*; Messrs. Methuen & Co. Ltd. for "In the Fashion" by A. A. Milne from *When We Were Very Young*; The Society of Authors and Mr. Geoffrey Dearmer for "The Whale"; the Proprietors of *Punch* for "The Watchmaker's Shop" by Elizabeth Fleming; Messrs. John Murray Ltd. for "Desolation" by Kao-Shih from *A Lute of Jade*; Messrs. Houghton Mifflin Company for "A Wish" by F. D. Sherman from *Little Folk Lyrics*; Messrs. Constable & Company Ltd. for "The Red Cockatoo" by Po Chiu, translated by Arthur Waley and taken from *170 Chinese Poems*; Jonathan Cape Limited and Mrs. H. M. Davies for "Sheep" and "The Cat" both from *The Collected Poems of W. H. Davies*; Messrs. Longmans Green & Co., Limited and representatives of the late Andrew Lang for "Chinook and Chinok" from *The Poetical Works of Andrew Lang*; Oxford University Press for "Kings Came Riding" by Charles Williams from *Modern Verse for Little Children* and "The Story of Augustus : by Heinrich Hoffman from *Struwwelpeter*; The Literary Trustees of Walter de la Mare and Messrs. Faber and Faber Ltd. for "Some One"; Miss Emily Lewis for her poem "My Dog"; Captain Francis Newbolt, C.M.G. for "Rilloby-Rill" by Sir Henr Newbolt from Poems New and Old published by Messrs.John Murra Ltd.; Messrs. Basil Blackwell & Mott Ltd. For "The Wind" by E. Rendall from *Thursday's Child*; Mr Wilfrid Gibson for his poems "Luck" and "The Parrots"; Messrs Macmillan & Co. Ltd. and the respetive authors for "The Snake and the Tortoise" by B. Lumsden Milne from *Modern Speech Rhythm Exercises* and "Fling Kites" by E. B. M. Watson from *Happy Speech*; Messrs Macmillan & Co. Ltd and Mrs J. Stephens for "Seumas Beg" from *Collected Poems of James Stephens*; Messrs Sidgwick & Jackson Ltd. For "Moonlit Apples" from *The Collected Poems of John Drinkwater*; Mrs B. P. Flexman for "W-o-o-o-ww" by Nancy M. Hayes; Mr. Thomas Mark for his poem "Hidden Treasure"; and Messrs.Wm. Collins, Sons & Co. Ltd. For "The Spider's Web" by Charlotte Druitt Cole.

In certain cases it has not been possible to trace the copyright holders, but full acknowledgement of any rights not mentioned here will be made in subsequent editions if notification is received.

To All Students

The poetry in this book has been chosen for you to read and enjoy.

Part One contains poems which you should find interesting to speak, either by yourself, or in groups arranged in different ways.

Part Two is called "Pictures in Poetry", because the poems in it describe scenes, persons and animals which, in some cases, will be familiar to you. After you have listened to a poem from Part Two, you might like to sketch or paint the pictures which you "see" in your mind.

Each of the poems in **Part Three** tells a story and you should be able to understand them with little difficulty. Some of the words, of course, will be new to you. But, with help, their meaning will soon become clear.

I hope you will enjoy the poems in this book so much that you will read more and more poems and perhaps make your own collection of favourites.

After reading and re-reading some of these poems and studying the way in which the poets have set to work, perhaps you will write some of your own?

To All Parents

It is pleasant to share interests and time with children. Poetry is often regarded as difficult. Some is difficult and some is not difficult. The poems in this series are carefully graded, with adequate notes to make reading pleasant and understanding accesible at levels suitable for each reader. Whether or not parents are already in the habit of reading poetry in English, they can enjoy reading the poems in this series of five books, with their children of all ages.

To All Teachers

This book contains a variety of poems of different degrees of difficulty to suit different ways of learning. The poems in Part One are suitable for reading aloud; those in Part Two are largely descriptive; and each poem in Part Three tells a story. The sequence in which the poems are used is, however, at the teacher's discretion.

The poems can be used as supplementary reading material, for oral work, including practice of stress and rhythm, and for different kinds of listening activities. The descriptive poems should develop and challenge the students' imagination and the 'story' or 'narrative' poems are included because all students like to hear or read a good story, provided that they can understand it. In addition to being enjoyed for themselves, the narrative poems provide material for choral work, for dramatization, discussions and questioning.

All the poems in this collection are suitable for extra-curricular work, for example, verse-speaking, choral-speaking, drama, and words and movement.

Poetry can be integrated successfully with the presentation and practice or activities stage of an English lesson, and if emphasis is placed on enjoyment and the students are encouraged to participate fully in the lesson, it can make learning more effective. Poetry develops and broadens the imagination through role-playing, provides training in visual perception, helps in the formation of ideas, and adds a new dimension to group work.

Poetry is an exploration of the possibilities of language which can help the student to construct a new and different framework from that of his own language, acquire different sequences and make forward guesses.

Poems to Speak

This section contains poems which have a pronounced rhythmic and musical quality and which are suitable for reading aloud, whether individually, or in chorus, or groups. Because it requires good breath-control, clear enunciation of consonants and precise shaping of vowels, choral speech is valuable as a way of training both ear and voice for all types of solo-speech. Whether a poem should be spoken by the class as a whole, by soloists, or by different groups of various sizes, depends upon the teacher's own preferences, and, even better, upon the ideas of the students themselves. When groups are required, it is a good idea to keep them constant for choral work in different lessons. In this way, it is possible to distribute the ablest speakers in the class among the various groups.

Some suggestions for choral arrangements are given in the Teaching/Learning Guide at the end of the book. Each poem which is at all suitable for choral work is, of course, open to much variation and the suggestions in the Guide should not therefore be taken as obligatory.

Pictures in Poetry

The poems in this section are intended to enhance the students' ability to visualise, in one form or another, what has been described. If the classroom environment is suitable, two or three poems can sometimes be read to create the right atmosphere for a lesson in which the aim is to encourage the students to sketch from the imagination. Once this atmosphere is achieved, the work can begin. When it is complete, the final results can be collected from individuals and shown to the rest of the group or class. Eventually, the students can be encouraged to make their own anthologies by writing out some of the poems from this collection and illustrating them from their own creative work. Pictures and photographs that are similar to scenes in the poems can be brought to the class to be used as the basis for discussion.

A Tale is Told

The poems in this section can be used as material upon which the students can comment and which they can use as the basis for writing their own stories in prose or verse on related themes. The success of the poetry-writing lesson will depend primarily upon the classroom atmosphere; and interruptions from outside the room should, therefore, be avoided as much as is possible. In the concluding stages of each lesson, the students can read their own poems aloud and be invited to make suggestions and comments.

The Teaching and Learning Notes and Guide

The Teaching and Learning Notes and Guide contain suggestions for choral arrangements; definitions and explanations of words and phrases; suggestions for illustration work and story-writing and questions for discussion.

Timeless and traditional

The books contain traditional and timeless poems, with abiding interest and usefulness. Literary techniques are introduced, including play on words (e.g. "Whether the Weather"), the use of assonance (a striking example is "Moonlit Apples"), alliteration, dialogue, onomatopoeia, refrain, repetition, rhyme, rhythm, the surprise ending. Much can be learnt from the narrative poems (e.g. the use of a sad ending ("The Princess Ming") and a happy ending ("Green Broom")).

The poems express and elicit many emotions – sympathy, concern, love, friendship, affection for people and creatures, loyalty (e.g. "The Lost Doll", "My Dog"), amusement, regret, sorrow, fear, wonder at the natural world and other people's behaviour, desire to be entertaining and useful ("The Toy-Man"). They demonstrate and encourage the use of the imagination (e.g. "A Child's Thought", "The Magic Room") and the thrills and discoveries that observation brings.

They introduce many personalities and varieties of personal interaction and teach the value and interest of putting oneself into the shoes of others (e.g. "The Fishes").

There are playful poems ("The Key of the Kingdom", which also teaches one way of ordering information; "This Old Man", which is also a number poem; "The Table and the Chair" which also encourages trying to do something out of the usual.) There are serious poems which make their point through imagery (e.g. "The Fountain").

A few are cautionary tales ("Three Little Children Sitting on the Sand" – do not trust strangers; "The Snake and the Tortoise" – boastfulness may be dangerous); "The Story of Augustus who would not have any Soup" – look after your health; "W-O-O-O-O-O-WW!" – learn from older and better informed people).

Information is conveyed (e.g. "The Sea Coral"). Discussion topics emerge naturally. For example, "Strange Talk" suggests the value of quiet; "Leave her, Johnnie" introduces attitudes to work; "A Man of Words" asserts that deeds are more valuable than words; "Where are you going to, my pretty maid?", "Feet and Paws" and "Hidden Treasure" each present different priorities and values.

The above points are examples only: each reader will find his or her own interest in these poems.

The audio recording (3rd edition only)

The audio recording gives examples of how two adult English native-speakers who enjoy reading aloud would read the poems. On another occasion, of course, they each might read the poems differently. There is no need to copy or ask students to copy their readings. However, these recordings will be useful in several ways. They will serve to make the meaning of the poems clearer. They offer interpretations of the poems and examples of the use of stress, pause, variety of pitch, enjambement and similar. They give good guidance as to the pronunciation of words that might be less familiar. They are enjoyable in themselves.

Variety may usefully be introduced in the use of the text and the recording. Sometimes, the text could be read first, sometimes the recording could be listened to first. Sometimes both could be used at the same time.

Write to us!

Teachers, students and parents are encouraged to write to us to share their experiences. We would be very interested to know which way of using this book and the related audio recordings was most useful to you. Please also let us know which particular poems your comments relate to. We look forward to hearing from you!

CONTENTS

PART ONE: POEMS TO SPEAK

PART TWO: PICTURES IN POETRY

PART THREE: A TALE IS TOLD

PART ONE

POEMS TO SPEAK

THE KEY OF THE KINGDOM

This is the Key of the Kingdom:
In that Kingdom there is a city;
In that city there is a town;
In that town there is a street;
In that street there winds a lane;
In that lane there is a yard;
In that yard there is a house;
In that house there waits a room;
In that room an empty bed;
And on that bed a basket.

A basket of sweet flowers,
of flowers, of flowers;
A basket of sweet flowers.

Flowers in a basket;
Basket on the bed;
Bed in the room;
Room in the house;
House in the weedy yard;
Yard in the winding lane;
Lane in the broad street;
Street in the high town;
Town in the city;
City in the Kingdom;
This is the key of the Kingdom.
Of the Kingdom this is the key.

Anonymous

LEAVE HER, JOHNNIE

Oh, the times are hard and the wages low—
    Leave her, Johnnie, leave her.
And now ashore again we'll go—
    It's time for us to leave her.

The grub was bad, the voyage long,
    Leave her, Johnnie, leave her.
The seas were high, the gales were strong,
    It's time for us to leave her.

She would not wear, she would not stay,
    Leave her, Johnnie, leave her.
She shipped it green, both night and day,
    It's time for us to leave her.

She would not stay, she would not wear,
    Leave her Johnnie, leave her.
She shipped it green and she made us swear,
    It's time for us to leave her.

The sails are furled, our work is done,
    Leave her, Johnnie, leave her!
And now ashore we'll take a run—
    It's time for us to leave her.

Sea Shanty

WHERE ARE YOU GOING TO, MY PRETTY MAID?

"Where are you going to, my pretty Maid?
Where are you going to, my pretty Maid?"

"I'm going a-milking, sir," she said,
"Sir," she said, "sir," she said.
"I'm going a-milking, sir," she said.

"May I go with you, my pretty Maid?
May I go with you, my pretty Maid?"

"You're kindly welcome, sir," she said,
"Sir," she said, "sir," she said.
"You're kindly welcome, sir," she said.

"What is your fortune, my pretty Maid?
What is your fortune, my pretty Maid?"

"My face is my fortune, sir," she said,
"Sir," she said, "sir," she said.
"My face is my fortune, sir," she said.

"Then I can't marry you, my pretty Maid,
Then I can't marry you, my pretty Maid."

"Nobody asked you, sir," she said,
"Sir," she said, "sir," she said,
"Nobody asked you, sir," she said.

Traditional

THREE LITTLE CHILDREN SITTING ON THE SAND

Three little children sitting on the sand,
All, all a-lonely,
Three little children sitting on the sand,
All, all a-lonely,
Down in the green wood shady—
There came an old woman, said "Come on with me,"
All, all a-lonely,
There came an old woman said, "Come on with me,"
All, all a-lonely,
Down in the greenwood shady—
She stuck her pen-knife through their heart,
All, all a-lonely,
She stuck her pen-knife through their heart,
All, all a-lonely,
Down in the green wood shady.

Anonymous

MIDNIGHT

Midnight's bell goes ting, ting, ting, ting, ting;
Then dogs do howl, and not a bird does sing
But the nightingale, and she cries twit, twit, twit:
Owls then on every bough do sit;
Ravens croak on chimney tops;
The cricket in the chamber hops,
And the cats cry mew, mew, mew.
The nibbling mouse is not asleep,
But he goes peep, peep, peep, peep, peep,
    And the cats cry mew, mew, mew,
    And still the cats cry mew, mew, mew.

Thomas Middleton

JOHN COOK

John Cook he had a little grey mare,
    Hee, haw, hum;
Her legs were long and her back was bare,
    Hee, haw, hum;
John Cook was riding up Shooter's Bank,
    Hee, haw, hum;
The mare she began to kick and prank,
    Hee, haw, hum;
John Cook was riding up Shooter's Hill,
    Hee, haw, hum;
His mare fell down and made her will,
    Hee, haw, hum;
The bridle and saddle were laid on the shelf,
    Hee, haw, hum;
If you want any more you may sing it yourself,
    Hee, haw, hum.

Anonymous

I SAW A PEACOCK

I saw a peacock with a fiery tail
I saw a blazing comet drop down hail
I saw a cloud wrapped with ivy round
I saw an oak creep upon the ground
I saw a pismire swallow up a whale
I saw the sea brimful of ale
I saw a Venice glass full fifteen feet deep
I saw a well full of men's tears that weep
I saw red eyes all of a flaming fire
I saw a house bigger than the moon and higher
I saw the sun at twelve o'clock at night
I saw the man that saw this wondrous sight.

Anonymous

STRANGE TALK

A little green frog lived under a log,
    And every time he spoke,
Instead of saying, "Good-morning,"
    He only said, "Croak-croak."

A duck lived by the waterside,
    And little did he lack,
But when we asked, "How do you do?"
    He only said, "Quack-quack."

A little pig lived in a sty,
    As fat as he could be,
And when he asked for dinner,
    He cried aloud, "Wee-wee."

Three pups lived in a kennel,
    And loved to make a row,
And when they meant, "May we go out?"
    They said, "Bow-wow! Bow-wow!"

If all these animals talked as much
    As little girls and boys,
And all of them tried to speak at once,
    Wouldn't it make a noise?

L. E. Yates

INFANT JOY

"I have no name:
I am but two days old."
What shall I call thee?
"I happy am,
Joy is my name."
Sweet joy befall thee!

Pretty joy!
Sweet joy, but two days old.
Sweet joy I call thee;
Thou dost smile,
I sing the while;
Sweet joy befall thee!

William Blake

A MAN OF WORDS

A man of words and not of deeds
Is like a garden full of weeds:
And when the weeds begin to grow,
It's like a garden full of snow;
And when the snow begins to fall,
It's like a bird upon the wall;
Ad when the bird away does fly,
It's like an eagle in the sky;
And when the sky begins to roar,
It's like a lion at the door;
And when the door begins to crack,
It's like a stick across your back;
And when your back begins to smart,
It's like a penknife in your heart;
And when your heart begins to bleed,
You're dead, and dead, and dead indeed.

Old Rhyme

DAPPLE GREY

I had a little pony,
    His name was Dapple-Gray,
I lent him to a lady,
    To ride a mile away.

She whipped him, she slashed him,
    She rode him through the mire;
I would not lend my pony now
    For all the lady's hire.

Traditional

WHETHER THE WEATHER

Whether the weather be fine,
Or whether the weather be not,
Whether the weather be cold,
Or whether the weather be hot,
We'll weather the weather,
Whatever the weather,
    Whether we like it or not.

Anonymous

THIS OLD MAN

This old man,
He played One,
He played nick-nack on my drum.
　Nick-nack, paddy whack,
　Give a dog a bone,
　This old man came rolling home.

This old man,
He played Two,
He played nick-nack on my shoe.
　Nick-nack, paddy whack,
　Give a dog a bone,
　This old man came rolling home.

This old man,
He played Three,
He played nick-nack on my knee.
　Nick-nack, paddy whack,
　Give a dog a bone,
　This old man came rolling home.

This old man,
He played Four,
He played nick-nack on my door.
　Nick-nack, paddy whack,
　Give a dog a bone,
　This old man came rolling home.

This old man,
He played Five,
He played nick-nack on my hive.
    Nick-nack, paddy whack,
    Give a dog a bone,
    This old man came rolling home.

This old man,
He played Six,
He played nick-nack on my sticks.
    Nick-nack, paddy whack,
    Give a dog a bone,
    This old man came rolling home.

Traditional

THE SEAL CORAL

O sailor, come ashore,
    What have you brought for me?
Red coral, white coral,
    Coral from the sea.

I did not dig it from the ground,
    Nor pluck it from a tree;
Feeble insects made it
    In the stormy sea.

Christina Rossetti

THE TABLE AND THE CHAIR

Said the Table to the Chair,
"You can hardly be aware
How I suffer from the heat,
And from chilblains on my feet!

"If we took a little walk
We might have a little talk!
Pray let us take the air,"
Said the Table to the Chair.

Said the Chair unto the Table,
"Now you *know* we are not able!
How foolishly you talk,
When you *know* we cannot walk!"

Said the Table with a sigh,
"It can do no harm to try;
I've as many legs as you,
Why can't we walk on two?"

So they both went slowly down,
And walked around the town,
With a cheerful, bumpy sound,
As they toddled round and round.

And everybody cried,
As they hastened to their side,
"See, the Table and the Chair,
Have come out to take the air!"

Edward Lear

HE AND SHE

He was a rat and she was a rat,
    And down in one hole they did dwell,
And both were as black as a witch's cat,
    And they loved one another well.

He had a tail, and she had a tail,
    Both long and curling and fine;
And each said, "Yours is the finest tail
    In the world, excepting mine."

He smelt the cheese, and she smelt the cheese,
    And they both pronounced it good;
And both remarked it would greatly add
    To the charms of their daily food.

So he ventured out, and she ventured out,
    And I saw them go with pain;
But what befell them I never can tell,
    For they never came back again.

Anonymous

THE SNAKE AND THE TORTOISE

A tortoise once upon a time
Lived very near a snake;
Each wanted, like a king, to rule
The swamp beside the lake.

This snake, he often tried to bite
The tortoise, but in vain;
Because the tortoise hid inside
His shell and felt no pain.

The tortoise laughed and said, "Ha! Ha!
You see I am the king
Of all this swamp, because I am
As strong as anything!"

"But why are you so very strong?"
The snake enquired. Then said
The tortoise: "It's because at sunset,
I cut off my head."

Then with a piece of wood he seemed
To cut his neck in two;
But really, he, both neck and head,
Into his shell withdrew.

The snake was very much impressed.
"But I've no feet," he said,
To hold the wood, I cannot think
What else to do, instead."

The tortoise answered kindly: "Bring
Your friends to-night with you;
The tortoises will come and lend

Their feet, the job to do."

So all the snakes came wriggling and
The tortoises as well;
They cut the heads off all the snakes
Because they had no shell.

The tortoises rejoiced. Their chief
Was king; and by the lake
Were many hundred tortoises
And not a single snake.

The moral of this little tale
Does not take long to tell,
To bite a tortoise never try,
Unless you have a shell!

B. Lumsden-Milne

THE OLD GREY GOOSE

Go and tell Aunt Nancy,
Go and tell Aunt Nancy,
Go and tell Aunt Nancy
The old grey goose is dead.

The one that she'd been saving
For to make her feather-bed.

She died last Friday
With a pain in all her head.

Old gander is weeping
Because his wife is dead.

The goslings are mourning
Because their mother's dead.

Anonymous

SNEEZING

Sneeze on Monday, sneeze for danger;
Sneeze on Tuesday, miss a stranger;
Sneeze on Wednesday, get a letter;
Sneeze on Thursday, something better;
Sneeze on Friday, sneeze for sorrow,
Sneeze on Saturday, see your sweetheart tomorrow.

Anonymous

THE FLY AND THE BUMBLE-BEE

Fiddle-de-dee, fiddle-de-dee,
The fly hath married the bumble-bee.
And all the birds of the air did sing,
"Have you ever seen so strange a thing?
Fiddle-de-dee, fiddle-de-dee,
The fly hath married the bumble-bee."

Anonymous

MEET-ON-THE-ROAD

"Now, pray, where are you going, child?" said Meet-on-the-Road.
"To school, sir, to school, sir," said Child-as-it-Stood.

"What have you got in your basket, child?" said Meet-on-the-Road.
"My dinner, sir, my dinner, sir," said Child-as-it-Stood.

"What have you for your dinner, child?" said Meet-on-the-Road.
"Some pudding, sir, some pudding, sir," said Child-as-it-Stood.

"Oh, then I pray, give me a share" said Meet-on-the-Road.
"I've little enough for myself, sir," said Child-as-it-Stood.

"What have you got that cloak on for?" said Meet-on-the-Road.
"To keep the wind and the cold from me," said Child-as-it-Stood.

"I wish the wind would blow through you," said Meet-on-the-Road.
"Oh, what a wish, Oh, what a wish!" said Child-as-it-Stood.

"Pray, what are those bells ringing for?" said Meet-on-the-Road.
"To ring bad spirits home again," said Child-as-it-Stood.

"Oh, then I must be going, child!" said Meet-on-the-Road.
"So fare you well, so fare you well," said Child-as-it-Stood.

Anonymous

THIS IS THE WAY

This is the way the ladies ride,
 Tri, tre, tre, tree,
 Tri, tre, tre, tree!
This is the way the ladies ride,
 Tri, tre, tri, tre, tri-tri-tree!

This is the way the gentlemen ride;
 Gallop-a-trot,
 Gallop-a-trot!
This is the way the gentlemen ride,
 Gallop-a-gallop-a-trot!

This is the way the farmers ride;
 Hobbledy-hoy,
 Hobbledy-hoy!
This is the way the farmers ride,
 Hobbledy-hobbledy-hoy!

Anonymous

THE WIND

I saw you toss the kites on high
And blow the birds about the sky;
And all around I heard you pass,
Like ladies' skirts across the grass—
    O wind, a-blowing all day long,
    O wind that sings so loud a song!

I saw the different things you did,
But always you yourself you hid.
I felt you push, I head you call,
I could not see yourself at all—
    O wind, a-blowing all day long,
    O wind that sings so loud a song!

O you that are so strong and cold,
O blower, are you young or old?
Are you a beast of field and tree,
Or just a stronger child than me?
    O wind, a-blowing all day long,
    O wind that sings so loud a song!

Robert Louis Stevenson

THE GOOD LITTLE GIRL

It's funny how often they say to me: "Jane?
    Have you been a *good* girl?
    Have you been a *good* girl?"
And when they have said it, they say it again:
    "Have you been a *good* girl?
    Have you been a *good* girl?"

I go to a party, I go out to tea,
I go to an aunt for a week at the sea,
I come back from school, or from playing a game;
Wherever I come from, it's always the same:
    "Well?
    Have you been a *good* girl, Jane?"

It's always the end of the loveliest day:
    Have you been a *good* girl?
    Have you been a *good* girl?"

I went to the Zoo and they waited to say:
    "Have you been a *good* girl?
Have you been a *good* girl?"

Well, what did they think that I went there to do?
And why should I want to be bad at the Zoo?
And should I be likely to say, if I had?
So that's why it's funny of Mummy and Dad,
This asking and asking, in case I was bad—
    "Well,
    Have you been a *good* girl, Jane?"

A. A. Milne

WHERE GO THE BOATS?

Dark brown is the river,
Golden is the sand,
It flows along for ever,
With trees on either hand.

Green leaves a-floating,
Castles of the foam,
Boats of mine a-boating:
Where will all come home?

On goes the river
And out past the mill,
Away down the valley,
Away down the hill.

Away down the river,
A hundred miles or more,
Other little children
Shall bring my boats ashore.

Robert Louis Stevenson

PART TWO

PICTURES IN POETRY

THE FISHES

Little silver fishes
    Darting to and fro,
I can see you shining
    As you come and go.

In the bright cool water
    Merrily you play.
That is very pleasant
    On a sunny day.

But, when winter passes
    Through this pretty glen,
Little silver fishes,
    What do you do then?

Lucy Diamond

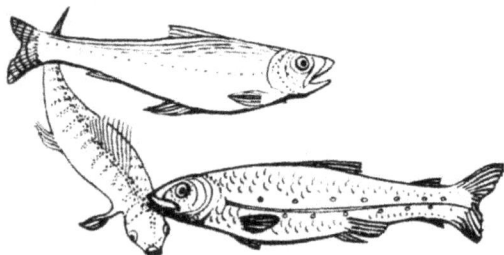

IF YOU HAVE A TABBY-CAT

If you have a tabby-cat,
    If you want to please him,
Tie a ribbon round his neck,
    Never, never tease him.
Tabby-cats are grave and stately,
    And they like to act sedately.

Agnes Grozier Herbertson

IS THE MOON TIRED?

Is the moon tired? She looks so pale
Within her misty veil;
She scales the sky from east to west,
And takes no rest.

Before the coming of the night
The moon shows papery white;
Before the dawning of the day
She fades away.

Christina Rossetti

THE SIX BLIND MEN OF HINDOSTAN

It was six men of Hindostan,
    To learning much inclined,
Who went to see the elephant
    (Though all of them were blind).
That each by observation
    Might satisfy his mind.

The first approached the elephant,
    And happening to fall
Against his broad and sturdy side,
    At once began to bawl,
"Bless me, it seems the elephant
    Is very like a wall".

The second, feeling of his tusk,
    Cried, "Ho! what have we hear
So very round and smooth and sharp?
    To me 'tis mighty clear
This wonder of an elephant
    Is very like a spear."

The third approached the animal,
    And happening to take
The squirming trunk within his hands,
    Then boldly up and spake;
"I see," quoth he, "the elephant
    Is very like a snake."

The fourth stretched out his eager hand
    And felt about the knee;
"What most this mighty beast is like
    Is mighty plain," quoth he;
"'Tis clear enough the elephant
    Is very like a tree."

The fifth who chanced to touch the ear
    Said, "Even the blindest man
Can tell what this resembles most;
    Deny the fact who can,
This marvel of an elephant
    Is very like a fan."

The sixth no sooner had begun
    About the beast to grope
Than, seizing on the swinging tail,
    That fell within his scope,
"I see," cried he, "the elephant
    Is very like a rope."

J. G. Saxe

FOUR BY THE CLOCK

Four by the clock! and yet not day;
But the great world rolls and wheels away,
With its cities on land, and its ships at sea,
Into the dawn that is to be!

Only the lamp in the anchored bark
Sends its glimmer across the dark;
And the heavy breathing of the sea
Is the only sound that comes to me.

H. W. Longfellow

A CHILD'S THOUGHT

At seven, when I go to bed,
I find such pictures in my head:
Castles with dragons prowling round,
Gardens where magic fruits are found;
Fair ladies prisoned in a tower,
Or lost in an enchanted bower;
While gallant horsemen ride by streams
That border all this land of dreams
I find, so clearly in my head
At seven, when I go to bed.

At seven, when I wake again,
The magic land I seek in vain;
A chair stands where the castle frowned,
The carpet hides the garden ground,
No fairies trip across the floor,
Boots, and not horsemen, flank the door,
And where the blue streams rippling ran

Is now a bath and water-can;
I seek the magic land in vain
At seven, when I wake again.

Robert Louis Stevenson

THE MAGIC ROOM

There's a room at the top of our house—
　　But it isn't a room to me;
It's an island surrounded with palms
　　And a whispering sea.

There's a room at the top of our house,
　　But it isn't a room to me;
It's a palace where I live alone,
　　With a magical key.

There's a room at the top of our house,
    But it isn't a room at all;
It's a cave where the treasures are kept
    In a wonderful wall.

There's a room at the top of our house,
    But it isn't really a room;
It's a castle built on a rock—
    Where the billows boom.

There's a room at the top of our house,
    But it isn't a room to me;
It's just whatever I choose—
    So it's magic, you see!

Irene Thompson

MOONLIT APPLES

At the top of the house the apples are laid in rows,
And the skylight lets the moonlight in, and those
Apples are deep-sea apples of green. There goes
    A cloud on the moon in the autumn night.

A mouse in the wainscot scratches, and scratches, and then
There is no sound at the top of the house of men
Or mice; and the cloud is blown, and the moon again
    Dapples the apples with deep-sea light.

They are lying in rows there, under the gloomy beams;
On the sagging floor; they gather the silver streams
Out of the moon, those moonlit apples of dreams,
    And quiet is the steep stair under.

In the corridors under there is nothing but sleep.
And stiller than ever on orchard boughs they keep
Tryst with the moon, and deep is the silence, deep
    On moon-washed apples of wonder.

John Drinkwater

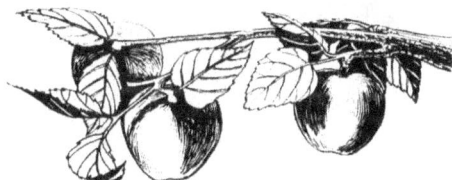

THE WINDING STAIR

Beware, beware
How you shall tread upon the stair.
Mark
How in the dark
The lightest footfall sounds,
And each soft tread
With unknown dread
The silence wounds.

Nor time nor care
Shall still the creaking stair,
But every step you take
Will wake
Within the breathing
gloom,
That to your listening ears
Is filled with whispered
fears,
A crack as loud as doom.

Upon the landing overhead
The watching clock with
sullen chime
Has summoned me to bed.
And I must climb
Through all the dark may own,
And what besides
Of haunted midnight hides,
The winding stair alone.

Anonymous

HOW DOTH THE LITTLE CROCODILE

How doth the little crocodile
  Improve his shining tail,
And pour the waters of the Nile
  On every golden scale!

How cheerfully he seems to grin,
  How neatly spreads his claws,
And welcomes little fishes in
  With gently smiling jaws!

Lewis Carroll

THERE IS A LADY SWEET AND KIND

There is a lady sweet and kind,
Was never face so pleas'd my mind;
I did but see her passing by,
And yet I love her till I die.

Her gesture, motion, and her smiles,
Her wit, her voice my heart beguiles,
Beguiles my heart, I know not why,
And yet I love her till I die.

Cupid is wingèd and doth range,
Her country so my love doth change:
But change she earth, or change the sky,
Yet I will love her till I die.

Anonymous

THE TOY-MAN

I'd like to be a toy-man
    And stand along the street,
And set my playthings working
    Beside the passing feet;
I'd wind them up and start them,
    And watch them run, and then
I'd pick them up and wind them,
    And start them off again.

So gay, and bright and lively
    My little pitch would be,
That everybody passing
    Would linger there to see;
And lots of grown-up people
    With little girls and boys
Would gather round my playground
    And buy my jolly toys.

Elisabeth Fleming

THE ELEPHANT

Here comes the elephant
Swaying along
With his cargo of children
All singing a song:
To the tinkle of laughter
He goes on his way,
And his cargo of children
Have crowned him with may.
His legs are in leather
And padded his toes;

He can root up an oak
With a whisk of his nose:
With a wave of his trunk
And a turn of his chin
He can pull down a house,
Or pick up a pin.
Beneath his grey forehead
A little eye peers!
Of what is he thinking
Between those wide ears?
Of what does he think?
If he wished to tease,
He could twirl his keeper
Over the trees:
If he were not kind,
He could play cup and ball
With Robert and Helen
And Uncle Paul:
But that grey forehead,
Those crinkled ears
Have learned to be kind
In a hundred years!
And so with the children
He goes on his way
To the tinkle of laughter
And crowned with the may.

Herbert Asquith

A VISIT FROM THE SEA

Far from the loud sea beaches
    Where he goes fishing and crying,
Here in the inland garden
    Why is the sea-gull flying?

Here are no fish to dive for;
    Here is the corn and the lea;
Here are the green trees rustling,
    Hie away home to sea!

Fresh is the river water
    And quiet among the rushes;
This is no home for the sea-gull,
    But for the rocks and the thrushes.

Pity the bird that has wandered!
    Pity the sailor ashore!
Hurry him home to the ocean,
    Let him come here no more!

High on the sea-cliff ledges
    The white gulls are trooping and crying;
Here among rocks and roses
    Why is the sea-gull flying?

Robert Louis Stevenson

THE PARROTS

Somewhere, somewhen I've seen,
But where or when I'll never know,
Parrots of shrilly green
With crests of shriller scarlet flying
Out of black cedars as the sun was dying
Against cold peaks of snow.

From what forgotten life
Of other worlds I cannot tell
Flashes that screeching strife;
Yet the shrill colour and shrill crying
Sing through my blood and set my heart replying
And jangling like a bell.

Wilfrid Gibson

THE TOAD AND THE FROG

"Croak!" said the Toad, "I'm hungry, I think;
To-day I've had nothing to eat or to drink;
I'll crawl to a garden and jump through the pales,
And there I'll dine nicely on slugs and on snails."
"Ho! ho!" quoth the Frog, "is that what you mean?
Then I'll hop away to the next meadow stream;
There I will drink, and eat worms and slugs too,
And then I shall have a good dinner like you."

Anonymous

THE WHALE

Wouldn't you like to be a whale
    And sail serenely by—
An eighty-foot whale from your tip to your tail
    And a tiny, briny eye?
Wouldn't you like to wallow
    Where nobody says "Come out!"
Wouldn't you *love* to swallow
    And blow all the brine about?
Wouldn't you like to be always clean
But never have to wash, I mean,
    And wouldn't you love to spout—
        O yes, just think—
    A feather of spray as you sail away
    And rise and sink and rise and sink
And blow all the brine about?

Geoffrey Dearmer

THE FOUNTAIN

Into the sunshine,
    Full of the light,
Leaping and flashing
    From morn till night!
Into the moonlight,
    Whiter than snow,
Waving so flower-like
    When the winds blow!
Into the starlight,
    Rushing in spray,
Happy at midnight,
    Happy by day!
Ever in motion,
    Blithesome and cheery,
Still climbing heavenward,
    Never a-weary;
Glad of all weather,
    Still seeming best,
Upward or downward
    Motion thy rest.
Full of a nature
    Nothing can tame,
Changed every moment,
    Ever the same;
Ceaseless aspiring,
    Ceaseless content,
Darkness or sunshine
    Thy element.
Glorious fountain!
    Let my heart be
Fresh, changeful, constant,
    Upward like thee!
J. R. Lowell

THE OLD MAN IN A BARGE

There was an old man in a barge,
Whose nose was exceedingly large;
    But in fishing by night,
    It supported a light,
Which helped that old man in a barge.

Edward Lear

IN THE FASHION

A lion has a tail and a very fine tail,
And so has an elephant, and so has a whale,
And so has a crocodile, and so has a quail—
    They've all got tails but me.

If I had sixpence I would buy one;
I'd say to the shopman, "Let me try one";
I'd say to the elephant, "This is my one!"
    They'd all come round to see.

Then I'd say to the lion, "Why, you've got a tail!
And so has the elephant, and so has the whale!
And, look! There's a crocodile! HE's got a tail!
    You've all got tails like me!"

A. A. Milne

I SAW A SHIP A-SAILING

I saw a ship a-sailing,
    A-sailing on the sea;
And, oh, it was all laden
    With pretty things for me!

There were comfits in the cabin,
    And apples in the hold;
The sails were made of silk,
    And the masts were made of gold.

The four-and-twenty sailors
    That stood between the decks,
Were four-and-twenty white mice,
    With chains about their necks.

The captain was a duck,
    With a jacket on his back;
And when the ship began to move,
    The captain said, "Quack! quack!"

Anonymous

THE WATCHMAKER'S SHOP

A street in our town
    Has a queer little shop
With tumble-down walls
    And a thatch on the top;
And all the wee windows
    With crookedy panes
Are shining and winking
    With watches and chains.

(All sorts and sizes
    In silver and gold,
And brass ones and tin ones
    And new ones and old;
And clocks for the kitchen
    And clocks for the hall,
High ones and low ones
    And wag-at-the-wall.)

The watchmaker sits
    On a long-legged seat
And bids you the time
    Of the day when you meet;
And round and about him
    There's tickety-tock
From the tiniest watch
    To the grandfather clock.

I wonder he doesn't
    Get tired of the chime
And all the clocks ticking
    And telling the time;
But there he goes winding
    Lest any should stop,
This queer little man
    In the watchmaker's shop.

From "Punch"

THE SAGE'S PIG-TAIL

There lived a sage in days of yore,
And he a handsome pig-tail wore;
But wondered much and sorrowed more,
Because it hung behind him.

Says he, "The mystery I've found;
I'll turn me round"—he turned him round;
But still it hung behind him.

Then round and round and out and in,
All day the puzzled sage did spin;
In vain—it mattered not a pin,
The pig-tail hung behind him.

And right and left and round about,
And up and down and in and out
He turned; but still the pig-tail stout
Hung steadily behind him.

And though his efforts never slack
And though he twist and twirl and tack,
Alas! still faithful to his back
The pig-tail hangs behind him.

W. M. Thackeray

A WISH

I often sit and wish that I
Could be a kite up in the sky,
And ride upon the breeze and go
Whatever way it chanced to blow;
Then I could look beyond the town,
And see the river winding down,
And follow all the ships that sail
Like me before the merry gale,
Until at last with them I came
To some place with a foreign name.

Frank Dempster Sherman

FROM A RAILWAY CARRIAGE

Faster than fairies, faster than witches,
Bridges and houses, hedges and ditches;
And charging along like troops in a battle,
All through the meadows the horses and cattle:
All of the sights of the hill and the plain
Fly as thick as driving rain;
And ever again, in the wink of an eye,
Painted stations whistle by.

Here is a child who clambers and scrambles,
All by himself and gathering brambles;
Here is a tramp who stands and gazes;
And there is the green for stringing the daisies!
Here is a cart run away in the road
Lumping along with man and load;
And here is a mill and there is a river:
Each a glimpse and gone for ever!

Robert Louis Stevenson

DESOLATION

There was a king of Liang—a king of wondrous might—
Who kept an open palace, where music charmed the night—

Since he was Lord of Liang a thousand years have flown,
And of the towers he builded yon ruin stands alone.

There reigns a heavy silence; gaunt weeds through windows
     pry,
And down the streets of Liang old echoes, wailing, die.

Kao-Shih

THE MOON

The moon has a face like the clock in the hall;
She shines on thieves on the garden wall,
On streets and fields and harbour quays,
And birdies asleep in the forks of the trees.

The squalling cat and the squeaking mouse,
The howling dog by the door of the house,
The bat that lies in bed at noon,
All love to be out by the light of the moon.

But of all the things that belong to the day
Cuddle to sleep to be out of her way;
And flowers and children close their eyes
Till up in the morning the sun shall rise.

Robert Louis Stevenson

THE RED COCKATOO

Sent as a present from Annam—
A red cockatoo
Coloured like the peach-tree blossom,
Speaking with the speech of men.

And they did to it what is always done
To the learnèd and eloquent.
They took a cage with stout bars
And shut it up inside.

Po-Chiu

SPACE TRAVELLERS

There was a witch, hump-backed and hooded,
    Lived by herself in a burnt-out tree.
When storm winds shrieked and the moon was buried
    And the dark of the forest was black as black,
    She rose in the air like a rocket at sea,
        Riding the wind,
        Riding the night,
    Riding the tempest to the moon and back.

There may be a man with a hump of silver,
    Telescope eyes and a telephone ear,
Dials to twist and knobs to twiddle,
    Waiting for a night when skies are clear,
    To shoot from a scaffold with a blazing track,
        Riding the dark,
        Riding the cold,
    Riding the silence to the moon and back.

James Nimmo

PART THREE

A TALE IS TOLD

THE PRINCESS MING

There was a prince by the name of Tsing,
    Who lived in the Chinese town of Lung
And fell in love with the Princess Ming,
    Who lived in the neighbouring town of Jung:
        'Twas a terrible thing
        For Tsing and Ming,
As you'll allow when you've heard me sing.

Now it happened so that the town of Lung,
    Where lived the prince who longed to woo,
Went out to war with the town of Jung
    With junks and swords and matchlocks too:
        'Twas a terrible thing
        For Tsing and Ming,
As you'll allow when you've heard me sing.

Miss Ming's papa was eating rice
    On yestermorn at half-past-eight,
And had carved a pie composed of mice,
    When the soldiers knocked at his palace gate;
        They were led by Tsing,
        And they called for Ming,
Which all will allow was a terrible thing.

Miss Ming's papa girt on his sword:
    "For this," quoth he, "I'll have his gore!"
In vain the Princess Ming implored—
    In vain she swooned on the palace floor—
        The Princess Ming
        Who was wooed by Tsing
Could not prevail with the gruff old King.

The old King opened the palace gate,
    And in marched Tsing with his soldiers grim,
And the King smote Tsing on his princely pate,
    Stating this stern rebuke to him:
        "It's a fatal thing
        For you, Mr Tsing,
To come a-courting the Princess Ming!"

The prince most keenly felt the slight,
    But still more keenly the cut on his head;
So suddenly turning cold and white,
    He fell on the earth and lay there dead:
        Which act of the King

To the handsome Tsing
Was a brutal shock to the Princess Ming.

No sooner did the young prince die
    Than Princess Ming from the palace flew
And jumped straight into the River Ji,
    With the dreadful purpose of dying too!
        'Twas a natural thing
        For the Princess Ming
To do for love of the handsome Tsing.

And when she leaped into the River Ji,
    And gasped and choked till her face was blue,
A crocodile fish came paddling by
    And greedily bit Miss Ming in two;
        The horrid old thing
        Devoured Miss Ming,
Who had hoped to die for the love of Tsing.

When the King observed her life adjourned
    By the crocodile's biting the girl in twain,
Up to the ether his toes he turned,
    With a ghastly rent in his jugular vein,
        So the poor old King,
        And Tsing and Ming
Were dead and gone—what a terrible thing!

And as for the crocodile fish that had
    Devoured Miss Ming in that dreadful way,
He caught the dyspepsy so dreadful bad
    That he too died that very day!
        So now, with the King,
        And Tsing and Ming,
And the crocodile dead, what more can I sing?

Eugene Field

THE ROBBERS

There was a man, and he had naught,
    And robbers came to rob him;
He crept up to the chimney top,
    And then they thought they had him.

But he got down on t'other side,
    And then they could not find him;
He ran fourteen miles in fifteen days,
    And never looked behind him.

Traditional

IN LONDON TOWN

It was a bird of Paradise,
    Over the roofs he flew.
All the children, in a trice,
Clapped their hands and cried, "How nice!
    Look—his wings are blue!"

His body was of ruby red,
    His eyes were burning gold.
All the grown-up people said,
"What a pity the creature is not dead,
    For then it could be sold!"

One was braver than the rest.
    He took a loaded gun;
Aiming at the emerald crest,
He shot the creature through the breast.
    Down it fell in the sun.

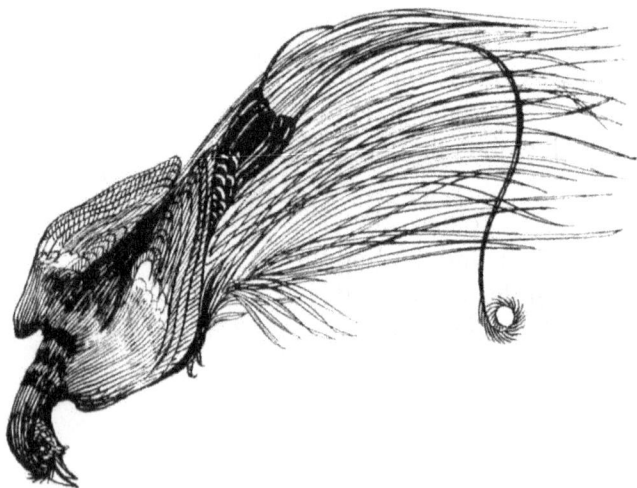

It was not heavy, it was not fat,
  And folk began to stare.
"We cannot eat it, that is flat!
And such outlandish feathers as that
  Why, who could ever wear?"

They flung it into the river brown.
  "A pity the creature died!"
With a smile and with a frown,
Thus they did in London town;
  But all the children cried.

Mary E. Coleridge

SHEEP

When I was once in Baltimore
  A man came up to me and cried,
"Come, I have eighteen hundred sheep,
  And we will sail on Tuesday's tide.   `

"If you will sail with me, young man,
  I'll pay you fifty shillings down;
These eighteen hundred sheep I take
  From Baltimore to Glasgow town."

He paid me fifty shillings down,
  I sailed with eighteen hundred sheep;
We soon had cleared the harbour's mouth,
  We soon were in the salt sea deep.

The first night we were out at sea
    Those sheep were quiet in their mind;
The second night they cried with fear—
    They smelt no pastures in the wind.

They sniffed, poor things, for their green fields,
    They cried so loud I could not sleep:
For fifty thousand shillings down
    I would not sail again with sheep.

W. H. Davies

THE CAT

Within that porch, across the way,
    I see two naked eyes this night;
Two eyes that neither shut nor blink,
    Searching my face with a green light.

But cats to me are strange, so strange—
    I cannot sleep if one is near;
And though I'm sure I see those eyes,
    I'm not so sure a body's there!

W. H. Davies

THE DUCK AND THE KANGAROO

Said the Duck to the Kangaroo,
   "Good gracious! how you hop!
Over the fields and the water too,
   As if you never would stop!
My life is a bore in this nasty pond,
     And I long to go out in the world beyond!
     I wish I could hop like you!"
     Said the Duck to the Kangaroo.

"Please give me a ride on your back!"
     Said the Duck to the Kangaroo.
"I would sit quite still, and say nothing but 'Quack',
     The whole of the long day through!
And we'd go to the Dee, and the Jelly Bo Lee,
     Over the land, and over the sea—
     Please take me a ride! O do!"
     Said the Duck to the Kangaroo.

Said the Kangaroo to the Duck,
     "This requires some little reflection;
Perhaps on the whole it might bring me luck,
     And there seems but one objection,
Which is, if you'll let me speak so bold,
     Your feet are unpleasantly wet and cold,
     And would probably give me the roo-
     Matiz!" said the Kangaroo.

Said the Duck, "As I sat on the rocks,
     I have thought over that completely,
And I bought four pairs of worsted socks
     Which fit my web-feet neatly.
And to keep out the cold I've bought a cloak,
     And every day a cigar I'll smoke,

All to follow my own dear true
    Love of a Kangaroo!"

Said the Kangaroo "I'm ready!
    All in the moonlight pale;
But to balance me well, dear Duck, sit steady!
    And quite at the end of my tail!"
So away they went with a hop and a bound,
And they hopped the whole world three times round;
    And who so happy—O who,
    As the Duck and the Kangaroo?

Edward Lear

SEUMAS BEG

A man was sitting underneath a tree
Outside a village and he asked me what
Name was upon this place, and said that he
Was never here before. He told a lot
Of stories to me, too. His nose was flat.
I asked him how it happened, and he said
The first mate of the *Mary Anne* done that
With a marling-spike one day, but he was dead.
And jolly good job, too; and he'd have gone
A long way to have killed him, and he had
A gold ring in one ear; the other one
"Was bit off by a crocodile, bedad."
That's what he said. He taught me how to chew.
He was a real nice man. He liked me, too.

James Stephens

CHICKS AND DUCKS

"The time is drawing very near,"
    Said Mrs Hen one day,
"For all my little chickens dear
    To break their shells away.
How proud and joyful I shall be
    When through the yard I go
With all my little family
    Behind me in a row."

Crack! go the eggs beneath her wings,
    Four little heads peep out,
And soon four fluffy little things
    Are running all about.

She leads them proudly through the yard,
    And gains the field beyond;
"For here," she thinks, "they're safe from harm,"
    When they espy a pond.

As fast as little legs can go
    They all start off. "Come back,
Come back, my dears," she cries in woe;
    They only answer, "Quack!"
"Alas! alas! they'll all be drowned;
They're in the pond," she clucks;
But, lo! they're swimming safe and sound,
    For they were all four ducks!

Anonymous

CHINOOK AND CHINOK

Chinook and Chinok were magicians of merit
Who each of them kept a familiar spirit;
They lived, we should tell you, a long while ago,
Between the Red Men and the wild Eskimo;
And the feats of the common magicians they'd mock,
Of the noisy Pow-wow, and the dark Angekok,
But the best of good friends were Chinook and Chinok!

It was nothing to either to fly in the air,
To float like a fish, or to climb like a bear.
It was nothing to either to change, by a wish,
His foes into fowls, and his friends into fish!
Thought Chinook, "I shall ask old Chinok to a feast,
And charm him, for fun, to the shape of a beast,
And when I have laughed at his fright till I'm black,
Why—dear old Chinok! I will alter him back."

So he sent to Chinok, and he asked him to dine.
Thought Chinok to himself, "I've an artful design,
For I'll change old Chinook to some sort of beast,
And I'll soon charm him back at the end of the feast!"

So they met, and their medicine-bags laid on the shelf;
But each had a powder he kept to himself—
A powder for making his friend look absurd
By changing him into a beast or a bird;
While each in his medicine-bag stored up another,
By which he'd restore his old shape to his brother.

Then both, when they settled serenely to eat,
Dropped a pinch of the powder unseen on the meat;
And Chinook, with a grin, began making his mock:
"Why, you're changing," he cried, "to a badger, Chinok!"
And Chinok, who felt rather uneasy, cried,
"Look, You are changing yourself to a toad, my Chinook!"

Then each of them longed to return to himself,
But the bags with the powders were high on the shelf;
And the badger can't climb, and the toad could not hop
To the shelf where the medicine-bags lay on the top;
So the pair could not reach them by hook or by crook,
And a badger and toad are Chinok and Chinook!

Yes, a toad and a badger those worthies remain,
And the moral of all is uncommonly plain,
That good luck never comes to a person who pokes
At a host, or a guest, his dull practical jokes!

Andrew Lang

THE STORY OF AUGUSTUS WHO WOULD NOT HAVE ANY SOUP

Augustus was a chubby lad;
Fat, ruddy cheeks Augustus had;
And everybody saw with joy
The plump and hearty, healthy boy.
He ate and drank as he was told,
And never let his soup get cold.

But one day, one cold winter's day,
He screamed out—"Take the soup away:
Oh, take the nasty soup away!
I won't have any soup today."

Next day begins his tale of woes,
Quite lank and lean Augustus grows.
Yet though he feels so weak and ill,
The naughty fellow cries out still—
"Not any soup for me, I say:
Oh, take the nasty soup away!
I won't have any soup to-day."

The third day comes; oh, what a sin!
To make himself so pale and thin.
Yet, when the soup is put on table,
He screams as loud as he is able,—
"Not any soup for me, I say:
Oh, take the nasty soup away!
I won't have any soup to-day."

Look at him, now the fourth day's come!
He scarcely weighs a sugar-plum;
He's like a little bit of thread,
And on the fifth day, he was dead!

Heinrich Hoffmann

GREEN BROOM

There was an old man and he lived in the West,
And his trade was the cutting of broom, green broom;
He had but one son, whose name it was John,
Who'd lie in his bed till noon, till noon,
Who'd lie in his bed till noon.

The old man arose and to his son goes,
And swore he would fire the room, the room,
If John wouldna rise and sharp up his knives
And go to the wood to cut broom, green broom,
And go to the wood to cut broom.

And John he arose and put on his clothes;
He banned and he swore and did fume, did fume,
To think that he should, with his breeding so good,
Be doomed all his life to cut broom, green broom,
Be doomed all his life to cut broom.

So John he passed on to the Greenwood alone,
Till he came to a castle of gloom, grey gloom;
He rapped at the gate where'er he could beat,
Crying, "Maids, will you buy my green broom, green broom?"
Crying, "Maids, will you buy my green broom?"

A lady on high did him then espy,
And marvelling much at his bloom, bright bloom,
She called on her maid to use all her speed
And bring up the youth with his broom, green broom,
And bring up the youth with his broom.

John climbed the dark stair without dread or fear,
Till he came to this fair lady's room, fine room;
With courtesy kind he pleased so her mind,
She asked him there for her groom, bride-groom,
She asked him there for her groom.

Now all ye broomcutters that live in the West,
Pray call at the castle of gloom, grey gloom;
There's both meat and drink, lads, and what do you think?
No trade like the cutting o' broom, green broom,
No trade like the cutting o' broom.

Traditional

OLD ROGER

Old Roger is dead and gone to his grave,
H'm, ha! gone to his grave.
They planted an apple tree over his head,
H'm, ha! over his head.

The apples grew ripe and ready to drop,
H'm, ha! ready to drop.
There came a high wind and blew them all off,
H'm, ha! blew them all off.
There came an old woman to pick them all up,
H'm, ha! pick them all up.
Old Roger got up and gave her a knock,
H'm, ha! gave her a knock.
Which made the old woman go hipperty hop,
H'm, ha! hipperty hop.

Anonymous

GREAT BIG DOG

Great big dog,
Head upon his toes;
Tiny little bee
Settles on his nose.

Great big dog
Thinks it is a fly.
Never says a word,
Winks very sly.

Tiny little bee,
Tickles dog's nose—

Thinks like as not
'Tis a pretty rose.

Dog smiles a smile,
Winks his other eye,
Chuckles to himself
How he'll catch a fly.

Then he makes a snap,
Very quick and spry,
Does his level best,
But doesn't catch the fly.

Tiny little bee,
Alive and looking well;
Great big dog,
Mostly gone to swell.

Moral:

Dear friends and brothers all,
Don't be too fast and free,
And when you catch a fly,
Be sure it's not a bee.

Anonymous

THE FROG AND THE BIRD

By a quiet little stream on an old mossy log,
Looking very forlorn, sat a little green frog;
He'd a sleek, speckled back, and two bright yellow eyes
And when dining, selected the choicest of flies.

The sun was so hot he scarce opened his eyes,
Far too lazy to stir, let alone watch for flies,
He was nodding, and nodding, and almost asleep,
When a voice in the branches chirped:
"Froggie, cheep, cheep!"

"You'd better take care," piped the bird to the frog,
"In the water you'll be if you fall off that log.
Can't you see that the streamlet is up to the brim?"
Croaked the froggie: "What odds! You forget I can swim!"

Then the froggie looked up at the bird perched so high
On a bough that to him seemed to reach to the sky;
So he croaked to the bird: "If you fall, you will die!"
Chirped the birdie: "What odds! you forget I can fly!"

Vera Hessey

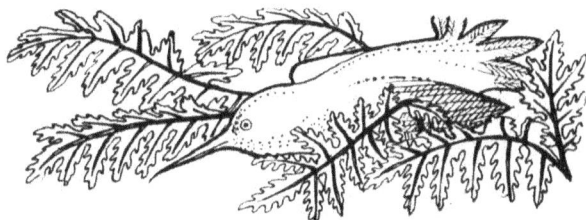

BETTY AT THE PARTY

"When I was at the party,"
    Said Betty, aged just four,
"A little girl fell off her chair
    Right down upon the floor;
And all the other little girls
    Began to laugh, but me—
I didn't laugh a single bit,"
    Said Betty seriously.

"Why not?" her mother asked her,
    Full of delight to find
That Betty—bless her little heart!—
    Had been so sweetly kind.
"Why didn't you laugh, my darling?
    Or don't you like to tell?"
"I didn't laugh," said Betty,
    "'Cause it was me that fell."

Anonymous

SOME ONE

Some one came knocking
 At my wee, small door;
Some one came knocking;
 I'm sure—sure—sure;
I listened, I opened,
I looked to left and right,
But nought there was a-stirring
 In the still dark night;
Only the busy beetle
 Tap-tapping in the wall,
Only from the forest
 The screech-owl's call,
Only the cricket whistling
 While the dew drops fall,
So I know not who came knocking,
 At all, at all, at all.

Walter de la Mare

DAYBREAK

A wind came up out of the sea,
And said, "O mists, make room for me."

It hailed the ships, and cried, "Sail on,
Ye mariners, the night is gone."

And hurried landward far away,
Crying, "Awake! it is the day."

It said unto the forest, "Shout!
Hang all your leafy banners out!"

It touched the wood-bird's folded wing,
And said, "O bird, awake and sing!"

And o'er the farms, "O chanticleer,
Your clarion blow; the day is near."

It whispered to the fields of corn,
"Bow down, and hail the coming morn."

It shouted through the belfry-tower,
"Awake, O bell! proclaim the hour."

It crossed the churchyard with a sigh,
And said, "Not yet! in quiet lie."

H. W. Longfellow

MY DOG

Have you seen a little dog anywhere about?
A raggy dog, a shaggy dog, who's always looking out
For some fresh mischief which he thinks he really ought to do,
He's very likely, at this minute, biting someone's shoe.

If you see that little dog, his tail up in the air,
A whirly tail, a curly tail, a dog who doesn't care
For any other dog he meets, not even for himself;
Then hide your mats, and put your meat upon the topmost
    shelf.

If you see a little dog, barking at the cars,
A raggy dog, a shaggy dog, with eyes like twinkling stars,
Just let me know, for though he's bad, as bad as bad can be;
I wouldn't change that dog for all the treasures of the sea.

Emily Lewis

LUCK

What bring you, sailor, home from the sea—
Coffers of gold and of ivory?

When first I went to sea as a lad
A new jack-knife was all I had:

And I've sailed for fifty years and three
To the coasts of gold and of ivory:

And now at the end of a lucky life,
Well, still I've got my old jack-knife.

Wilfrid Gibson

MY SHADOW

I have a little shadow that goes in and out with me,
And what can be the use of him is more than I can see;
He is very, very like me from the heels up to the head,
And I see him jump before me, when I jump into my bed.

The funniest thing about him is the way he likes to grow—
Not at all like proper children, which is always very slow;
For he sometimes shoots up taller like an india-rubber ball,
And he sometimes gets so little that there's none of him at all.

He hasn't got a notion of how children ought to play,
And can only make a fool of me in every sort of way.
He stays so close beside me, he's a coward you can see,
I'd think shame to stick to nursie as that shadow sticks to me!

One morning very early, before the sun was up,
I rose and found the shining dew on every buttercup;
But my lazy little shadow, like an arrant sleepy-head,
Had stayed at home behind me and was fast asleep in bed.

Robert Louis Stevenson

THE WIND

Why does the wind so want to be
Here in my little room with me?
He's all the world to blow about,
But just because I keep him out
He cannot be a moment still,
But frets upon my window sill.
And sometimes brings a noisy rain
To help him batter at the pane.

Upon my door he comes to knock.
He rattles, rattles at the lock
And lifts the latch and stirs the key—
Then waits a moment breathlessly,
And soon, more fiercely than before,
He shakes my little trembling door,
And though, "Come in, Come in!" I say,
He neither comes nor goes away.

Barefoot across the chilly floor
I run and open wide the door;
He rushes in and back again
He goes to batter door and pane,
Pleased to have blown my candle out.
He's all the world to blow about,
Why does he want so much to be
Here in my little room with me?

E. Rendall

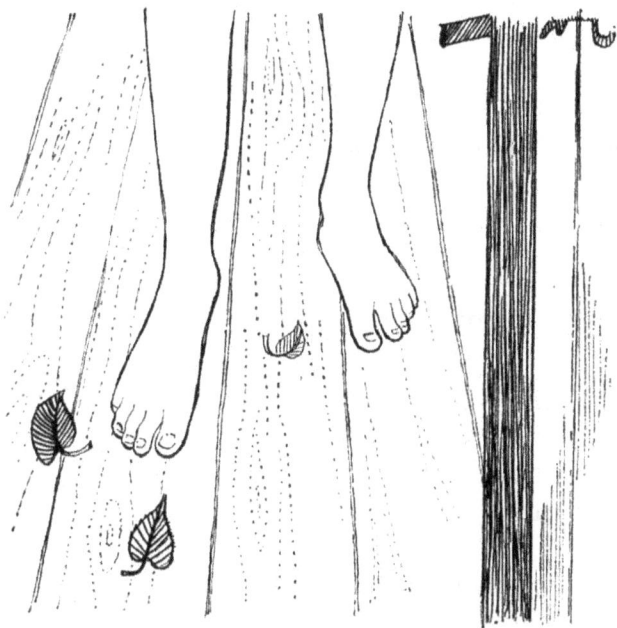

THE LOST DOLL

I once had a sweet little doll, dears,
    The prettiest doll in the world;
Her cheeks were so red and so white, dears,
    And her hair was so charmingly curled.
But I lost my poor little doll, dears,
    As I played in the heath one day;
And I cried for her more than a week, dears;
    But I never could find where she lay.

I found my poor little doll, dears,
    As I played in the heath one day;
Folks say she is terribly changed, dears,
    For her paint is all washed away,
And her arms trodden off by the cows, dears,
    And her hair not the least bit curled:
Yet for old sakes' sake she is still, dears,
    The prettiest doll in the world.

Charles Kingsley

HIDDEN TREASURE

They told me there was treasure in my garden,
    If I'd only take a spade and dig;
And there wasn't much to measure in my garden,
    For it wasn't very big.

So I gave some of my leisure to my garden,
    And I dug it well from end to end;
But I didn't find the treasure in my garden—
    Or none that I could spend!

Yet I got a lot of pleasure from my garden,
    When the flowers grew thick and tall:
So perhaps that was the treasure in my garden
    After all!

Thomas Mark

W-O-O-O-O-O-WW!

Away in the forest all darksome and deep
The Wolves went a-hunting when men were asleep:
And the cunning Old Wolves were so patient and wise
As they taught the young Cubs how to see with their eyes,
How to smell with their noses and hear with their ears
And what a Wolf hunts for and what a Wolf fears.
Of danger they warned: "Cubs, you mustn't go there—
It's the home of the Grizzily-izzily Bear."
        W-o-o-o-o-o-ww!

The Cubs in the Pack very soon understood
If they followed the Wolf law the hunting was good.
And the Old Wolves who'd hunted long winters ago
Knew better than they did the right way to go.
But one silly Cub thought he always was right
And he settled to do his own hunting one night.
He laughed at the warning—said he didn't care
For the Grizzily-izzily-izzily Bear!
        W-o-o-o-o-o-ww!

So, when all his elders were hot on the track,
"I'm off now!" he barked to the Cubs of the Pack.
"I'll have some adventures—don't mind what you say!"
A wave of his paw—and he bounded away.
He bounded away till he came very soon,

Where the edge of the forest lay white in the moon,
To what he'd been warned of—that terrible lair—
The haunt of the Grizzily-izzily Bear!
　　W-o-o-o-o-o-ww!

He came . . . and what happened? Alas! To the Pack
That poor silly Wolf-cub has never come back.
And once, in a neat little heap on the ground,
The end of a tail and a whisker were found,
Some fur and a nose-tip—a bristle or two,
And the kindly old Wolves shook their heads, for they knew
It was all of his nice little feast he could spare,
That Grizzily-izzily-izzily Bear!
　　W-o-o-o-o-o-ww!

Nancy M. Hayes

FEET AND PAWS

Feet and paws run in and out,
　　In and out all day,
Leaving dusty tracks about,
　　Everywhere they play;
Kitchen, corridor, and stair,
　　Sitting room and hall,
Feet and paws without a care
　　Tread them one and all.

Though so often brush and mop
　　Follow in their track,
No one orders them to stop,
　　No one calls them back;
No one grumbles while they go
　　Where they will, because

Everybody loves them so,
  Little feet and paws!

Elisabeth Fleming

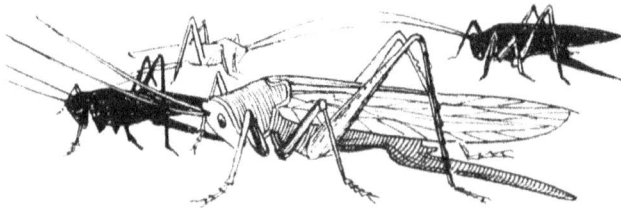

RILLOBY-RILL

Grasshoppers four a-fiddling went,
  Heigh-ho! never be still!
They earned but little towards their rent,
But all day long with their elbows bent
  They fiddled a tune called Rilloby-rilloby,
  Fiddled a tune called Rilloby-rill.

Grasshoppers soon on Fairies came,
Heigh-ho! never be still!
  Fairies asked with a manner of blame,
"Where do you come from, what is your name?
  What do you want with your Rilloby-rilloby,
  What do you want with your Rilloby-rill?"

"Madam, you see before you stand,
  Heigh-ho! never be still!
The Old Original Favourite Grand
Grasshoppers Green Herbarian Band,
  And the tune we play is Rilloby-rilloby,
  Madam, the tune is Rilloby-rill."

Fairies hadn't a word to say,
    Heigh-ho! never be still!
Fairies seldom are sweet by day,
But the Grasshoppers merrily fiddled away,
    Oh, but they played with a willoby-willoby,
    Oh, but they played with a willoby-will!

Fairies slumber and sulk at noon,
    Heigh-ho! never be still!
But at last the kind old motherly moon
Brought them dew in a silver spoon,
    And they turned to ask for Rilloby-rilloby,
    One more round of Rilloby-rill.

Sir Henry Newbolt

QUEEN MAB

A little fairy comes at night,
    Her eyes are blue, her hair is brown,
With silver spots upon her wings,
    And from the moon she flutters down.

She has a little silver wand,
    And when a good child goes to bed
She waves her hand from right to left,
    And makes a circle round its head.

And then it dreams of pleasant things
    Of fountains filled with fairy fish,
And trees that bear delicious fruit,
    And bow their branches at a wish:

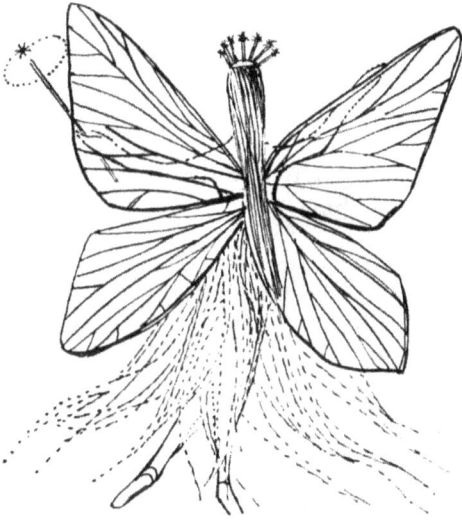

Of arbours filled with dainty scents
    From lovely flowers that never fade;
Bright flies that glitter in the sun,
    And glow-worms shining in the shade;

And talking birds with gifted tongues
    For singing songs and telling tales,
And pretty dwarfs to show the way
    Through fairy hills and fairy dales.

But when a bad child goes to bed,
    From left to right she weaves her rings,
And then it dreams all through the night
    Of only ugly, horrid things!

Thomas Hood

THE WITCH

I don't know how she came into the room—
    I didn't see her broom;

The two dogs saw her, whisking here and there,
    And howled with bristling hair.

It can't have been much more than half-an-hour,
    Yet all the milk went sour.

Silence was everywhere, and her black cat,
    My heart went pit-a-pat.

Then she went up the chimney on a flame—
    Perhaps the way she came!

Caron Rock

TEACHING AND LEARNING NOTES AND GUIDE
BOOK TWO

PART ONE: POEMS TO SPEAK

THE KEY OF THE KINGDOM

This poem is very suitable, to introduce children to the idea of choral work and might occupy the class for several lessons. The teacher should give a preliminary reading and illustrate to the children by his or her own performance how a climax can be achieved in the last lines of each verse. Various lines can then be given to the students, to read aloud. One child, for example, can be asked to say the first line himself, another child can join him in the reading of the second line, three children can read the third and the cumulation of voices can continue until, 'a basket of sweet flowers'. The process can then be effectively reversed until the first speaker has the last line of the second verse to himself. Other variations will suggest themselves to the teacher as the class becomes more familiar with the poem.

LEAVE HER, JOHNNY

A selected group of children or the teacher can narrate the story, whilst the rest of the class speaks the refrain:

'Leave her, Johnny, leave her,
It's time for us to leave her.'

Alternatively, different individual groups of two or three children could take each line of the refrain separately whenever it occurs.

grub	slang term for food.
shipped it green	the sea flooded the decks.
furled	rolled up.

WHERE ARE YOU GOING TO, MY PRETTY MAID?
After a first reading by the teacher, half the class can speak the lines of the young man, whilst the other half gives the pretty maid's answers.

THREE LITTLE CHILDREN
This rather tragic little nursery rhyme can be effectively dramatised, whilst at the same time it is useful for choral work and provides good practice for the improvement of the initial consonant sound s. One suitable choral arrangement after the teacher's first reading would be for a small group to say lines 1, 3, and 5, and just the words, 'There came an old woman, said', in lines 6 and 8. One student could speak the second half of lines 6 and 8 ('Come on with me') and a second selected group could say lines 10, 11, 13, and 15. The remainder of the class might read the refrain, 'All, all a-lonely'. After this arrangement has been practised two or three times, four students could be chosen to take the parts of the three little children and the old woman. The scene and actions suggested by the story might then be mimed, whilst the reading is taking place.

MIDNIGHT
For listening practice, as the teacher reads the poem to the class twice. Later, various students can be asked to read the poem individually.

JOHN COOK
Another useful traditional nursery-rhyme for choral work. Many variations are possible. One suggestion is for the teacher to tell the sad tale of John Cook whilst all the children in the class speak the refrain. If possible, the children should be shown by the teacher's example that there are four beats in each line, except that the last one in the refrain ('Hee, haw,

hum' . . .) is 'silent'. After some repetition the children might perceive this for themselves.

I SAW A PEACOCK
Each line can be read by a different student. After two readings in this way, the teacher can ask the students to add a semicolon after the first noun in each line. Different punctuation will be found to have altered the sense of the poem and it can now be read a third time by the teacher, who, by observing the new pauses, can stress the change of meaning.

pismire　　a very old word for an ant.

A MAN OF WORDS
Individual students or small groups can speak the first line, whilst the rest of the class speaks the second line, of each couplet. The last line of the poem can be said lugubriously by the whole class.

STRANGE TALK
Whilst the teacher narrates this poem, the children can imitate the sounds of the various animals where appropriate.

INFANT JOY
One student could speak lines 1, 2, 4, and 5 of the first verse, whilst the teacher takes line 3 and line 6. In the second verse, one student could say the first line, another student the 'Sweet joy' of line 2, the rest of the class reading the second half ('but two days old') of this line. Lines 3, 4, and 5 can be read by the teacher and the last line of the poem by the whole class. This poem provides a change from the typical rhythms to be found in most poems commonly used in the early years in the Primary School.

befall　　　　　　happen to.

Sweet joy befall thee!   may you have sweet joy.

DAPPLE GRAY
The actions in this nursery-rhyme could be mimed whilst half the class says the first verse and the other half the second. Children can take it in turns to mime the characters of the boy or girl, the pony and the lady.

WHETHER THE WEATHER
Most useful to practise the consonant w and for lipping practice. The 'h' in 'wh' need not be sounded. The whole class could, with advantage, speak this together.

THIS OLD MAN
Several variations are possible for the reading of this traditional nursery rhyme. The teacher can narrate the story in each verse whilst the children repeat the refrain, or different groups of students can tell the story, whilst the rest of the class speaks the refrain. If the children can then be taught to sing the usual tune associated with these verses, so much the better.

THE SEA CORAL
The teacher can ask the question in the first two lines; half the class can say 'Red coral' and the other half 'White coral', whilst a selected group speaks the last line of the first verse. One individual student can take line one of the second verse, another might speak line two, and the whole class can say the last two lines of the poem. The teacher might bring a piece of coral to show the children, if this is available.

THE TABLE AND THE CHAIR
One child can speak the part of the Table and another the part of the Chair. The whole class could say line one of verse one, line four of verse two, and line one of verses three and four. Four separate groups might speak each of the lines of the fifth

verse and the whole class could take the first two lines of the last verse. The last two lines could be given to a group of, say, five children. This poem provides useful practice for 'sem' (ow as in 'now'), 'i:' (ee as in 'seat') and 'ei' (ay as in 'rain', 'say').

HE AND SHE

This poem offers scope both for planned and improvised dramatisation, whilst speaking is going on. The teacher can narrate the poem whilst the children mime its story, and other groups, under the teacher's guidance, can speak the lines. In a mixed class, for example, the first lines of each stanza could be given to a girl and a boy—the girl to say the first half of the line, the boy the second. Three other groups can be responsible for the remaining lines in each set of four, excepting stanza two, where the dialogue could perhaps be spoken by another soloist. Other variations are possible for a class of boys or girls.

THE SNAKE AND THE TORTOISE

The teacher can speak the first two verses and the narrative portions of the other verses of the poem. One student can say the part of the tortoise and another the part of the snake. Different groups of children can be encouraged to mime the various events of the story as they are told.

THE WIND

A suitable poem for the teacher to read aloud to the children except for the refrain in each verse, which the students could say together.

THE GOOD LITTLE GIRL

After a first reading by the teacher, several individual students can be asked to come out and read the poem in turn. The teacher can then read it again himself, whilst the class listens.

WHERE GO THE BOATS?
Four groups could say a verse each. When selecting the groups the teacher might look for 'light', 'medium', and 'heavy' voices and experiment with different arrangements of them.

THE OLD GREY GOOSE
Lines one to three of verse one could be said by three different individual students and line four by the whole class together. Verses two, three, four, and five might then be spoken by four separate groups.

SNEEZING
Good for practice of the combination sound 'sn' and also the vowel 'i:' (ee as in 'meet'). One group could say the first half of each line, whilst a second group completes it.

THE FLY AND THE BUMBLE-BEE
One group might speak the first and the second lines. The whole class could take the third line and a second group, the fourth. The whole class again could speak lines 5 and 6. This poem can be used to practise the 'i:' sound (ee as in 'meet').

MEET-ON-THE-ROAD
One student or small group could speak the part of Meet-on-the-Road, whilst another student or group says the lines of Child-as-it-Stood. The teacher could speak the narrative sections. This poem might occupy three or four lessons and different pairs of children could take it in turn to mime the meeting of the two characters.

THIS IS THE WAY
This nursery-rhyme is very useful for general articulation work and for particular practice of the 'ai' sound (i as in 'fight', 'my') and 'i:' (ee as in 'seat', 'meet'). The teacher could speak each

line beginning, 'This is the way', whilst individual students or groups take the other lines in turn.

PART TWO: PICTURES IN POETRY

THE FISHES
After reading the poem to the class, the teacher can encourage discussion. The word 'glen' (narrow valley) will require some explanation. After the discussion, the teacher might read one or two other poems of a similar theme (for example, 'Fishes', Book One, page 12, or 'The Goldfish', Book One, page 42) and then, after suitable material has been provided, ask the children to draw or paint a picture about fish.

IF YOU HAVE A TABBY CAT
A simple little poem very suitable for illustration. tease: to worry and make fun of. grave: serious. stately: dignified. sedately: composedly, free from hurry or agitation.

IS THE MOON TIRED?
The teacher can read two other poems, entitled 'The Moon', from Book One, page 14, and Book Two, page 72, to introduce children to the theme. 'Is the Moon Tired?' can then be read aloud by the teacher, a short discussion can be held and drawing and painting can follow.
scales: moves across.

THE SIX BLIND MEN OF HINDOSTAN
The teacher should first of all narrate the poem to the class. A discussion and questions might follow, such as:

1. Why did the first blind man think the elephant was like a wall?
2. Why did the third man think the elephant was like a snake?

3. What did the sixth man do when he came near to the elephant?
4. Which part of the elephant did the fifth man touch?
5. Why was each of the six blind men 'partly in the right' and partly wrong?

sturdy	not easily knocked down; firm.
squirming	wriggling like a worm.
quoth	said.
resembles	to be like; have similarity to.
grope	search blindly.
disputed	argued.

After the discussion the poem could be read aloud a second time by the teacher. Individual students, however, could speak the parts of the six blind men. In later lessons, the children can be asked to draw or paint the scene they imagine, after a further reading.

FOUR BY THE CLOCK
One or two readings by the teacher should be followed immediately by drawing and painting.

bark	sailing ship.
glimmer	faint light.

A CHILD'S THOUGHT
After reading the poem two or three times, the teacher can ask half the class to draw or paint what they 'see' after listening to the first verse. The other half can be asked to do the same for verse two. When this work is complete, the pictures can be discussed and the best efforts exhibited on the classroom wall.

flank   are near to the magic room

After the preliminary reading by the teacher, the class can speak the first line of each verse together, whilst the teacher reads the poem again. A discussion and questions can follow and then each child can be asked to draw or paint his own 'magic room'.

MOONLIT APPLES
The poem should be read to the class two or three times (the teacher's reading will need thorough preparation) and then discussion and questions can follow.

skylight   glazed opening in a roof.
wainscot   boarding or panelling on a wall.
dapples   varies with rounded spots of colour or shade.
sagging   sinking unevenly.

This poem has been included for illustration work. Each verse provides material for a different picture.

THE WINDING STAIR
The students can draw and paint the scenes they 'see' after the teacher has read the poem two or three times.

HOW DOTH THE LITTLE CROCODILE
An appropriate little poem for illustration work.

golden   a thin horny plate protecting the skin of the
scale   crocodile. (The poet imagines it to be golden in
        colour.)

THERE IS A LADY SWEET
A good class can be asked to listen to the teacher's reading of this poem and a discussion can follow.

beguiles   charms, delights.

THE TOY-MAN

After the teacher's first reading and some discussion, individual students may be asked to read the poem in turn. The teacher could bring to the classroom several of the mechanical toys often sold by street hawkers and, after the children's reading, these can be wound up and made to work. When all the children have seen them and the excitement has died down, drawing and painting may begin.

THE ELEPHANT

After the teacher has read the poem to the students two or three times, there should be some discussion to ensure that the content has been thoroughly understood. Crowned him with may: in England, May is a month associated with flowers and greenery and the first day of the month is a country festival. A girl is often chosen to be 'Queen' for this one day and, as a rule, she is given a 'crown' made of blossom called 'hawthorn', or 'may'.

twirl   twist or spin round quickly.

A VISIT FROM THE SEA

This poem should be read by the teacher two or three times. A discussion and questions can then follow, for example:
1. Where has the sea-gull come from?
2. Where is he now?
3. Why does the poet think the gull should fly back to the ocean?
4. What are the white gulls doing over the sea-cliffs?
inland: interior of country away from the sea.

lea	piece of 'meadow' land
hie	go quickly!
rushes	Marsh plants with long, thin, stems
rook	a kind of bird

Drawing and painting from the imagination can follow the discussion.

THE PARROTS
The teacher might create interest by reading one or two other short poems to the children first. Two readings of The Parrots might follow and then, without further explanation, the children can be asked to illustrate what they 'see'. In a lesson of this type all materials (paints, brushes, paper, etc.) must be prepared beforehand.

shrilly   dazzling

THE TOAD AND THE FROG
Whilst the teacher reads the narrative sections, individual students can take turns to speak the parts of the Toad and the Frog. Drawing and painting can follow the oral work.
pales: wooden stakes serving as part of a fence.

THE WHALE
A useful poem for illustration work. One or two readings by the teacher and a brief discussion might precede the picture-making.

briny   salty ('brine' is salt water).

The imaginative illustrations will have to stem from the children's own reading rather than from experience and the teacher, therefore, should not expect to see whales that look like whales! It is the imaginative effort which matters and no marks of any kind should be awarded to the students' work.

THE FOUNTAIN
With a good fourth year class, the teacher should read this
poem two or three times. A discussion should then take place,
followed by picture-making.

blithesome	gay, joyous
aspiring	reaching upward
constant	continuous

The more significant ideas of the poem (for instance, the poet's
desire to be like the fountain) should be ignored by the teacher
at this stage.

THE OLD MAN IN A BARGE
This poem provides a useful introduction to 'nonsense' poetry.
The teacher will probably find that he has to spend more time
in preparatory work with poems of this kind, than with those
which make sense. Children whose mother tongue is not
English often find humour of the type written by poets like
Lear, Carroll and Belloc difficult to appreciate at first,
although a little preliminary discussion often clarifies the
difficulties and the poetry is then thoroughly enjoyed.

IN THE FASHION
The teacher can narrate this poem except for the child's Words
which may be spoken by an individual student. After a short
discussion, the class can be asked to draw or paint pictures of
elephants, crocodiles, whales and lions!

quail   a type of bird

I SAW A SHIP A-SAILING
Suitable for imaginative picture-making after reading and
discussion.
comfits   sweets

THE WATCHMAKER'S SHOP
After a preliminary reading, the teacher might initiate a discussion about the type of watchmaker's shop to be found in the students' own country. The children could then be asked to draw and paint pictures from their own experience.

thatch	roofing of straw and rushes.
grandfather clock	a type of clock in a tall wooden case that stands on the floor.

THE SAGE'S PIG-TAIL
This poem should be read aloud to the class by the teacher two or three times. A discussion and questions could then follow, for instance:
1. What did the sage find strange about his pig-tail?
2. Why did he turn round and round?
3. Why did the pig-tail continue to hang behind the sage?

sage	wise man.
mused upon this curious case	wondered thoughtfully why the pigtail hung behind him.

A WISH
After a reading and discussion of this poem, students could be encouraged to write their own brief poems beginning, 'I wish . . .

FROM A RAILWAY CARRIAGE
The teacher should read the poem aloud to the children, maintaining the train-like rhythm as he speaks. Questions can follow, such as:
1. What can be seen in the meadows as the train passes by?
2. What does the child do? (Or, more difficult, 'What is the child doing?')

3. Who stands and gazes? (or, again more difficult, 'Who is standing and gazing?')
4. What does the whistling—the station or the train? (the last line of verse one).

After the preliminary questions, the children can be led to a simple discussion of the poem's structure. The teacher can help by asking questions which test the students' imagination, for example:

1. (To an individual student) You are the tramp standing in the field. What do you see when you look at the railway line?
2. (To another student) You are the same tramp. What do you hear as the train approaches?
3. (To a third student) You are looking out of one of the train's carriage windows. What do you see on the road?
4. Is it raining? What 'fly as thick as driving rain'?
5. What are 'charging along like troops in a battle'?

daisy   A very common English flower. (Children often string them together to make pretty necklaces.)

DESOLATION
A useful poem to test the comprehension ability of a good fourth year class. If the poem is read effectively and the right atmosphere is carefully built up, some interesting picture-making might result.

THE MOON
The teacher might read one or two other 'moon poems' first to prepare the children for his reading of The Moon. Drawing and painting of what the children have 'seen' can then begin.

THE RED COCKATOO
A discussion of the meaning of this little poem can follow the teacher's reading. The children might then be asked to attempt sketches of the cockatoo if the bird is a native of their country.

eloquent   fluent speaker.

SPACE TRAVELLERS
The teacher should read the poem to the class twice. A
discussion can follow and questions can be asked:
1. Where did the witch live?
2. What did the witch look like?
3. How do you think the witch rode to 'the moon and back'?
4. What was the weather like during the witch's journeys?
5. What sort of weather will the 'man' wait for?
6. What is the scaffold? (launching platform).
7. Where will the 'man' go?
After the discussion, the poem can be read again and then half
the class can be asked to illustrate the first verse whilst the
remainder of the class illustrates the second verse. The best
'witches' and 'spacemen' can be pinned on the classroom
display boards.

PART THREE: A TALE IS TOLD

THE PRINCESS MING
The teacher can read through the poem twice to give the
children a general idea of the story. Words that are new to
them can then be mentioned and written on the blackboard in
the context of sentences. A general discussion may then follow
and the teacher can initiate this by asking a number of
questions:
1. Where did Prince Tsing live?
2. Who lived in the town of Jung?
3. Who killed Prince Tsing?
4. What did Princess Ming do when she heard that Prince
Tsing was dead?
5. What happened to Princess Ming in the river?
6. When did the crocodile die?

7. What did he die of?

matchlock	an old gun.
girt	put on.
swooned	fainted.
could not prevail	could not make him change his mind.
pate	head.
slight	insult.
adjourned	had come to an end.
in twain	in two.
ether	sky.
jugular vein	a large vein in the neck.
dyspepsy	indigestion, stomach-ache.

THE ROBBERS
A simple little story poem.

naught	nothing.
t'other	the other (shortened slang form).

IN LONDON TOWN
After the teacher's first reading, the class can join in speaking
the dialogue as the teacher narrates. A discussion and
questions can then follow:
1. Where did the bird fly?
2. Why did the grown-up people wish the creature was dead.
3. How did the 'braver' man kill the bird?
4. Why didn't the people want to eat the bird?
5. What did the people eventually do with the bird?
6. Why did all the children cry?

in a trice	at once.
emerald crest	bright green tuft or comb on the bird's head.
outlandish	unfamiliar and strange.

SHEEP
Two readings by the teacher may be followed by discussion
and questions:
1. How much was the young man paid to sail with the sheep?
2. How many sheep were there?
3. What did the sheep do on the second night out at sea?
4. What familiar smells did the sheep miss?
After the discussion, the poem can be read again and a group
of students might read the lines spoken by the man.

THE CAT
A strange little poem. The teacher may ask students what they
make of it.

porch   covered approach to the entrance of a building.

THE DUCK AND THE KANGAROO
The teacher's first reading can be followed by choral-work by
the children. One child can say the lines of the Duck and
another those of the Kangaroo. The rest of the class can repeat
the story-teller's lines whenever they occur, i.e. 'Said the Duck
to the Kangaroo', 'Said the Kangaroo to the Duck'; 'Said the
Duck', etc.

Jelly Bo Lee	a fictitious nonsensical name.
reflection	thought.
roo-Matiz	playful rendering of the word, "rheumatism".
worsted	woollen.

SEUMAS BEG
The teacher can read the poem to the children, and afterwards
they might be asked to write a prose description of the sailor or,
if they wish, sketch or paint a picture of him.

Seumas   pronounced Shay-muss.

marling-	marline-spike, a pointed tool used for opening
spike	strands of rope so that two ends can be spliced or
	joined together.

CHICKS AND DUCKS
Children can take it in turn to speak the part of Mrs Hen and the teacher can say the storyteller's lines. A discussion and questions may follow two or three readings, for example:
1. How many eggs were there?
2. Where did Mrs Hen lead the 'four little things'?
3. What did 'the little things' do when they saw the pond?
4. Why was Mrs Hen frightened?
5. Why didn't the four 'little things' drown?

CHINOOK AND CHINOK
The teacher might speak the story whilst individual students in turn say the lines of Chinook and Chinok. A discussion can follow two or three readings and some questions such as the following will help the children to understand the poem:
1. What were Chinook and Chinok?
2. Into what creatures did they often change their foes?
3. Where did Chinook and Chinok put their medicine-bags whilst they were feasting?
4. Why couldn't Chinook and Chinok change themselves back by magic?
5. What is the lesson to be learned from this story?

familiar spirit	a demon who served him.
Pow-wow	an American medicine-man, similar to a
	Witchdoctor, or magician.
Angekok	Eskimo medicine-man.
artful	cunning.
absurd	foolish.
serenely	calmly.
making his	making fun of (Chinok).

mock	
by hook or by crook	no matter how much they tried.
worthies	persons.

THE STORY OF AUGUSTUS
Whilst the teacher reads the storyteller's lines, the children can speak the part of Augustus. This poem might be used by the teacher to provide a suggestion for original writing by the class. The children can be asked to write a short poem on similar or related themes, e.g. 'Over-eating'. In a lesson of this type it is important for the teacher to give the students plenty of freedom to choose their own topic and their own style. Some poems might be in rhyme, whilst others may hardly be distinguishable from prose. It is the imaginative effort which matters.

GREEN BROOM
The teacher's reading may be followed by questions and a discussion, for example:
1. What was the old man's trade?
2. Why did the old man say he would 'fire' John's room?
3. What happened after John had rapped at the castle gate?
4. What did the lady do when she met John?

broom	a shrub with yellow flowers which grows on sandy soil.
wouldna	would not.
banned	cursed.
fume	showing anger.

OLD ROGER
Very suitable for choral work. The teacher, separate groups, or individual students can read the first, third, fifth, seventh, ninth, eleventh, and thirteenth lines, whilst the rest of the class speak the alternate lines together.

GREAT BIG DOG
This simple story (or narrative) poem gives the teacher an opportunity to explain to the class what is meant by 'a story with a moral'. A moral attached to a story, whether in the form of poetry or prose, explains to the reader what can be learned from that story.

THE FROG AND THE BIRD
The teacher's first reading can be followed by another reading in which the class can participate. Two separate groups could speak the lines of the Frog and the Bird.

forlorn   sad, forsaken.
sleek   soft and smooth.

BETTY AT THE PARTY
The class can join in the reading of this poem. One student can speak Betty's lines and another might take the part of the mother. The teacher can narrate the rest of the poem.

SOME ONE
After listening to the teacher's reading of this poem, children may be encouraged to sketch or paint what they 'see'. This little story poem can also be used as an example to be read before the students write on a similar theme.

DAYBREAK
The wind from the sea delivers different messages to the ships, forest, birds, farms, etc. Whilst the teacher narrates most of the poem, the wind's messages can be spoken by different individual students.

chanticleer   cockerel, male chicken.

MY DOG
As the teacher reads the poem, three different groups can speak the second line in each of the three verses. These lines provide useful practice of the 'ae' (a as in 'sat') and the a: (ir as in 'bird') sounds. After the reading the children might be asked to write a poem of their own on the subject of 'My Dog'. The poems produced could later be illustrated by the students' own drawings and paintings.

LUCK
After the teacher's first reading, half the class might speak line 1 and the other half line 2. The teacher can then speak the remainder of the poem.

coffers   big boxes in which valuables are kept.

MY SHADOW
The preliminary reading can be followed by a short discussion and questions, for example:
1. Why is the shadow very, very like the storyteller?
2. Why does the shadow stay so close beside the storyteller?
3. What did the story-teller find one morning after rising before the sun was up?
4. What had the shadow done that morning?

buttercup   a yellow English flower that grows wild.
arrant   downright, blunt, frank.

THE WIND
This poem can be read by the teacher to provide the class with an example before they begin to write their own poems on the same subject.

frets   worries.

THE LOST DOLL
After the teacher's reading, the children could be asked to draw or paint two pictures each—one of the doll as described in the first verse and one of the doll as described in the second verse.

heath   a flat piece of waste land often covered with shrubs

HIDDEN TREASURE
The teacher's reading might be followed by a discussion leading to the central question, 'What was the treasure?' Careful hard work and digging during some of the poet's leisure time made the garden fertile and the flowers grew well.

W-O-O-O-O-O-WW!
Whilst the teacher reads most of this poem, the class can join in by speaking the 'W-o-o-o-o-o-ww!' in each verse. A discussion of the lesson to be learned from the poem can follow a series of questions, such as:
1. Where did the wolves hunt?
2. Name one thing the Old Wolves taught the Cubs.
3. What did the silly young Cub decide to do on his own?
4. Where was the Grizzly Bear's lair?
5. What happened to the silly Wolf-cub?

darksome   dark.
lair   den.

FEET AND PAWS
This poem can be read to the students as an example before they begin writing themselves.

RILLOBY-RILL
This poem can be spoken by different sections of the class. The teacher can read lines 1, 3, and 4 of verse one, whilst one

student speaks line 5, and another student speaks line 6. In verse two, the teacher can speak lines 1 and 3, the whole class can say line 4, and the same individual students can speak lines 5 and 6. Four students can say the grasshoppers' lines in verse three (lines 1, 3, 4, 5, and 6). In the fourth verse, the teacher can take lines 1, 3, and 4, whilst one student speaks line 5 and another student line 6. In the last verse of the poem, the teacher can take lines 1, 3, and 4, whilst in a grand climax the whole class may speak the last two lines in chorus. The refrain (line 2 of each verse of the poem) may be spoken by all the class throughout. This poem provides very useful practice of the 'r' sound, used initially.

QUEEN MAB
After the teacher has read the poem to the class, a discussion can be held and questions asked:
1.What is the colour of the fairy's eyes?
2. What is the colour of her hair?
3. What does she do when a good child goes to bed?
4. When does the fairy come?
5. What do the dwarfs do?
6. What does the fairy do when a bad child goes to bed?
7. What does the bad child dream about?
After this, the children could be asked to write down some of the pleasant things they would like to dream about.

THE WITCH
After listening to the teacher's reading of this poem, the children can be encouraged to write their own poems about the same or a similar subject. The poem also evokes a scene which can be illustrated.

ABOUT THE EDITOR

Verner Bickley is an educationist who has led international education projects in Singapore, Burma, Indonesia, Japan, Saudi Arabia and Hong Kong. For two years, he was Chairman of Directors of the East-West Centre in Hawaii and, for ten years, was Director of the Centre's Culture Learning Institute. He has served as an adjudicator in speech and drama festivals in several countries and as President of the English-Speaking Union in Hawaii and Chairman of the English-Speaking Union in Hong Kong. He has lived and worked in Hong Kong since 1983.

Specialising in institutional linguistics, language pedagogy and international education, Dr Bickley has written extensively on language and culture and on language learning and teaching. He has served as announcer and actor in radio and TV programmes broadcast in several Asian and Pacific countries. His voice was heard regularly over the NHK in Tokyo, the Burma Broadcasting Service, Radio Republic Indonesia and Radio Malaya where he broadcast from Singapore as newsreader and as actor and narrator in radio drama, as well as in programmes for schools and colleges.

Among the dozens of scripts he has written were five in a series on the use of poetry in the language class, broadcast in BBC radio's "Listen and Teach" series. Twenty scripts written by Dr Bickley for the Japan Broadcasting Company were broadcast as the television series, "How English Works".

His books include *Reading and Interpretation* (co-authored), *Reading and Understanding* (co-authored), *A New Malayan Songbook* (co-authored), *Easy English*, *Cultural Relations in the Global Community*, *Searching for Frederick* (an autobiographical-biographical narrative), *Language and the Young Learner in Hong Kong,* and *Forward to Beijing*. The first volume of his autobiography entitled, *Footfalls Echo in the Memory*, was published in 2010, and the second volume, *Steps to Paradise and Beyond: Hawaii to China, Saudi Arabia, Hong Kong and Elsewhere*, in 2013.

Born in Cheshire, England, Dr Bickley received two bachelor's degrees from the University of Wales, before earning an M.A. degree in education there. He was made a Licentiate of the Royal

Aademy of Music (Speech and Drama) in 1955 and a Licentiate of the Guildhall School of Music and Drama in the same year. He was awarded a PhD in socio-linguistics by the University of London in 1966. He is a Fellow of the Royal Society of Arts.

Employed by the British Council for twelve years, he moved from university teaching and advisory assignments to the position of English Language Officer for Japan and First Secretary in the Cultural Department of the British Embassy in Tokyo.

Dr Bickley was founding Director of the Hong Kong Government's Institute of Language in Education (which was incorporated into the Hong Kong Institute of Education after his retirement) and an Assistant Director of Education.

Dr Bickley was made a Member of the Order of the British Empire in 1964.

ABOUT PROVERSE HONG KONG

Proverse Hong Kong, co-founded by Gillian and Verner Bickley, is based in Hong Kong, with growing regional and international connections. Verner Bickley has headed cultural and educational centres, departments, institutions and projects in many parts of the world. Gillian Bickley has recently concluded a career as a university teacher of English Literature, spanning four continents. Proverse Hong Kong draws on their combined academic, administrative and teaching experience as well as varied long-term participation in reading, research, writing, editing, reviewing, publishing and authorship.

Proverse Hong Kong has published novels, novellas, single author short story collections, non-fiction (including memoirs, biography, war and travel diaries and journals, fictionalised autobiography, history, sport), single-author poetry collections, editions of nineteenth-century writing, academic and young teen books. Other interests include academic works in the humanities, social sciences, cultural studies, linguistics and education. Some Proverse books have accompanying audio texts. Proverse editors work with texts by non-native-speaker writers of English as well as by native English-speaking writers.

Proverse welcomes authors who have a story to tell, wisdom, perceptions or information to convey, a person they want to memorialise, a neglect they want to remedy, a record they want to correct, a strong interest which they want to share, skills they want to teach, and who consciously seek to make a contribution to society in an informative, interesting and well-written way.

The name, *Proverse*, combines the words "prose" and "verse" and is pronounced accordingly.

SOME EDUCATIONAL BOOKS FROM PROVERSE

Jockey, by Gillian Bickley (when Gillian Workman). Hong Kong, 1979. Pbk. 64pp.
ISBN-10: 962-85570-3-3; ISBN-13: 978-962-85570-3-5.

Poems to Enjoy: Book 1, Edited by Verner Bickley. HK & UK: 2012. Pbk. 136 pp. (inc. 35 b/w original line-drawings & Teacher's and Student's Notes). With audio CDs. ISBN 978-988-8167-54-8.

Poems to Enjoy: Book 2, Edited by Verner Bickley. HK & UK: 2013. Pbk. 136pp. (inc. 37 b/w original line-drawings & Teacher's and Student's Notes). With audio CDs. ISBN 978-988-8167-51-7.

Poems to Enjoy: Book 3, Edited by Verner Bickley. HK & UK: 2013. Pbk. 166 pp. (inc. 39 b/w original line-drawings & Teacher's and Student's Notes). w. audio CDs. ISBN 978-988-19934-1-0.

Poems to Enjoy: Book 4, Edited by Verner Bickley. HK & UK: scheduled, 2014. Pbk. *c.*174 pp. (inc. *c.*41 b/w original line-drawings & Teacher's and Student's Notes).
With audio CDs. ISBN 978-988-8167-50-0.

Poems to Enjoy: Book 5, Edited by Verner Bickley. HK & UK: scheduled, 2015. Pbk. *c.*200 pp. (inc. *c.*36 b/w original line-drawings & Teacher's and Student's Notes).
With audio CD(s) / DVD(s). ISBN 978-988-8167-49-4.

Spanking Goals and Toe Pokes: Football Sayings Explained, by T. J. Martin. HK & UK, 2008. ISBN-13: 978-988-99668-2-9.

Teachers' and Students' Guide to the Book and Audio Book, 'The Golden Needle: the Biography of Frederick Stewart (1836-1889)'. Proverse Hong Kong Study Guides. E-book. ISBN-10: 962-85570-9-2; ISBN-13: 978-962-85570-9-7. 24Reader e-book edition (2010), ISBN-13: 978-988-19320-5-1.

THE PROVERSE INTERNATIONAL LITERARY PRIZES

THE INTERNATIONAL PROVERSE PRIZE

The Proverse Prize, an annual international competition for an unpublished single-author book-length work of fiction, non-fiction, or poetry, the original work of the entrant, submitted in English (translations are welcome) was established in January 2008. It is open to all who are at least eighteen on the date they sign the entry form and without restriction of nationality, residence or citizenship.

The objectives of the prize are: to encourage excellence and / or excellence and usefulness in publishable written work in the English Language, which can, in varying degrees, "delight and instruct". Entries are invited from anywhere in the world.

Entry forms available each year from	No later than 14 April
Closing date for entry forms, fees and entered work	30 June
Judging	July-September
Semi-finalists announced	No later than November

THE INTERNATIONAL PROVERSE POETRY PRIZE (SINGLE POEMS)

Entry forms, entry fees, and entered work received from	7 May
Closing date for entry forms, fees and entered work	30 June
Judging	July-September
Winners announced	No later than November

More information, updated from time to time, is available on the Proverse Hong Kong website: proversepublishing.com

Poems to Enjoy: Book Two (Fifth Edition) 133

FIND OUT MORE ABOUT PROVERSE AUTHORS BOOKS AND EVENTS

Visit our website:
http://www.proversepublishing.com
Visit our distributor's website: www.chineseupress.com

Follow us on Twitter
Follow news and conversation: <twitter.com/Proversebooks>
OR
Copy and paste the following to your browser window and
follow the instructions:
https://twitter.com/#!/ProverseBooks

"Like" us on www.facebook.com/ProversePress
Request our free E-Newsletter
Send your request to info@proversepublishing.com.

Availability

Most books are available in Hong Kong and world-wide
from our Hong Kong based Distributor,
The Chinese University Press of Hong Kong,
The Chinese University of Hong Kong, Shatin, NT,
Hong Kong SAR, China.
Email: cup-bus@cuhk.edu.hk
Website: www.chineseupress.com

All titles are available from Proverse Hong Kong
http://www.proversepublishing.com
and the Proverse Hong Kong UK-based Distributor.

We have stock-holding retailers in Hong Kong,
Canada (Elizabeth Campbell Books),
Andorra (Llibreria La Puça, La Llibreria).
Orders can be made from bookshops
in the UK and elsewhere.

Ebooks
Most of our titles are available also as Eb